D0774967

everyday
raw gourmet

matthew kenney
photographs by miha matei

GIBBS SMITH
TO ENRICH AND INSPIRE HUMANKIND

First Edition
17 16 15 14 13   5 4 3 2 1

Text © 2013 Matthew Kenney
Photographs © 2013 Miha Matei

Published by
Gibbs Smith
P.O. Box 667
Layton, Utah 84041

1.800.835.4993 orders
www.gibbs-smith.com

Designed by Debra McQuiston
Printed and bound in Hong Kong

Gibbs Smith books are printed on paper produced
from sustainable PEFC-certified forest/controlled
wood source. Learn more at www.pefc.org.

Library of Congress Cataloging-in-Publication Data

Kenney, Matthew.
[Entertaining in the raw]
Everyday raw gourmet / Matthew Kenney ;
photographs by Miha Matei. — Revised edition.
pages cm
Revision of author's Entertaining in the raw. 2009.
Includes index.
ISBN 978-1-4236-3480-5
1. Cooking (Natural foods) 2. Raw foods. 3.
Entertaining. 4. International cooking. I. Title.
TX741.K46 2013
641.3'02—dc23
2013003798

contents

the goal of life is living in agreement with nature.

—Zeno (335–264 BC)

introduction

Create—The first time I stepped into a raw food kitchen, I knew that I had discovered something magical. My senses had been on high alert as I remained deeply suspicious about uncooked food, and many years in professional kitchens had created a foundation of principles contrary to what I was about to experience. Yet I nearly became an instant convert, ready to forgo not only fire and heat but also the majority of ingredients that were the building blocks of my cuisine.

To this day, I still remain captivated by steaming pots of risotto, the hearty aromas of a wood-fired oven, and the intense flavor brought on by a long-simmering reduction. Yet nothing has ever captured my attention in a kitchen like the crisp smell of fresh ginger mingling with coriander and lime, as I entered that day. And nothing has held it like the explosive clean flavor of well-prepared raw organic foods.

My first year of preparing raw was somewhat challenging. Just as I was entering a phase of my career where the skills I had learned and experiences I had accumulated should have provided me with the tools I needed to cook at a higher, more mature level, I chose to discard everything and begin anew. Fortunately, it was a natural decision, taken not only for professional and creative reasons but also in light of my own personal preferences, which had begun to lean more and more toward a plant-based lifestyle. The choice led me to the most rewarding and creative experience of my life.

In the beginning, just as with traditional European-based cuisine, it was necessary to learn the basics. Instead of stocks and bases, searing and braising, I needed to experiment with Brazil nut milk and vegetable juice–based sauces and to focus on marinating and dehydrating as ways to intensify flavor. There were a few triumphs and many failures; but as I experimented more, dishes began to emerge that would open up a raw food world of unlimited potential. Over the next two years, I would begin to delineate two styles of raw food preparation: practical dishes that are faster to prepare at home or for a quick meal, and more elaborate dishes that require a bit more patience and effort. Those more elaborate dishes are largely what make raw food so remarkable. The health benefits and flavors of everyday raw food are incredible on many levels. As a chef, I am most inspired by the tastes, textures, and presentation of the more advanced recipes.

There is no denying that some of the best raw food dishes are downright challenging to prepare. Several steps may be involved, often beginning with "sprouting" nuts, seeds, or grains, and ending with as much as forty-eight hours of dehydration. Others may provide a bit more instant gratification. This book is written in honor of the more elaborate, but very worthwhile, recipes that challenge the cook and please the guest. The attention, persistence, and care that go into the recipes in this book deserve to be celebrated and enjoyed by those who are fortunate enough to eat them.

Share—In my earlier days with raw food, I often found myself shying away from preparing it for family and friends, instead finding a middle ground with perhaps vegetarian or vegan dishes. Over time, as my food evolved, I became more confident about people's reaction to this incredible cuisine, and now I prepare it whenever I have the opportunity. Whether it be a simple raw lunch or an exquisite tasting menu, the impact and pleasures of raw food are, by and large, incomparable to other challengers.

No other culinary style offers the same vibrant, deep flavor without guilt or other effects that gourmet foods often have, such as a heavy feeling or fatigue. Raw food is the most colorful on the planet—it literally jumps off the plate! Raw is very modern, forgoing heavy sauces, dairy products, and breads, allowing each bite to pack maximum flavor. In every one of my raw dining experiences, I have found that the food ends up not only being enjoyed but also being used as a conversational piece, where guests marvel at their surprise to learn the food before them is composed of fruits, vegetables, nuts, and seeds, none of which have been cooked, canned, or processed in any way.

Some of the ideas are pretty "out there"—think Willy Wonka's chocolate or Andy Warhol's art factory, where unbounded creativity exists in an effort to pursue meaning and, in this case, the essence of raw food. My philosophy is guided by one stipulation: all of the culinary efforts shall be devoted to preparing the most advanced, flavorful, and realistic raw food anywhere. As long as my work considers those fundamental issues, I allow pretty much free reign to spontaneously experiment and create. The results should entertain not only guests but also the cook.

It is always a good idea to consider the balance of dishes that are served. My chapters provide some guidance in this area and highlight ways that food can be combined to make a statement beyond just taste. All of the recipes in this book are inspired by a season, emotion, or other value that relates to experimental cuisine. I believe that food for entertaining is more interesting if it relates to something larger, just as the best art and literature always offer a message beyond their respective beauty or story. A menu concept can be as straightforward as "summer" and as elaborate as something inspired by contemporary art. These concepts also provide more for guests to indulge in and will surprise the cook in how they also give a deeper appreciation for the food itself. Whereas French cuisine, for example, has centuries of history behind it, upscale raw food is relatively new, and these creative attachments help build its core personality.

Enjoy—As a home or professional cook, perhaps the greatest reward with this food is that you will have a better opportunity to be with your guests, because the food does not have to be warmed, reduced, heated, and taken out of the oven. Assuming the mis en place is taken care of, assembly is still required, but it will be much faster than usual to finalize the plates. Most of these recipes are not portioned in a traditional way, meaning that they provide the flexibility to be served on smaller plates or larger platters or, in most cases, at a large decorated table. They hold up well and many don't need to be eaten right away. Having no pots and pans to wash is perhaps the final surprise.

On my own journey with raw food, I found challenge, excitement, flavor, health, and a new sense of creative direction. If this book offers you the same rewards, I think you'll be well fed—and happy.

Guidance—Every book has a story—where its idea originated, what the message is, and how it should be used on a day-to-day basis. In writing this one, although the book has developed a personality of its own over time, my goal has always been to bring to life the many unique possibilities that raw food beholds. I am so personally impressed by raw food, and inspired on a regular basis, that I instinctively knew the kind of book I wanted to write from the beginning. Putting the words and recipes together was a far more complicated process, but it still happened naturally. The result is a very personal expression of how raw food fits into our daily lives, not only from a culinary but also an emotional perspective. In order to use *Raw Gourmet* most effectively, it would be beneficial to adapt your own personal approach to the information it offers. Allow my recipes and suggestions to serve as a guideline, always remembering that you are the chef in your kitchen. I offer a few suggestions as to how you may enjoy your experience even more.

Recipes are like roadmaps: They may offer the fastest way to arrive at a result, but your trip must take into account personal tastes, your schedule and sometimes even the weather. Although I may like something spicy, you may prefer it a bit sweet, or a dish that I've recommend you serve in a composed manner might be more appealing to you with its components kept separate. Time is something that we all value and never seem to have enough of. Therefore, it is always necessary with detailed recipes such as these, to read a recipe in its entirety, think about your approach and make decisions about what can be done ahead, of if there is a component you'd like to leave out. My comment about the weather is a very real one: humidity or dryness affects the texture of many raw food recipes and can dramatically alter dehydrating times, crispness, and even taste of some dishes. An ingredient in one part of the world may look the same but taste totally different than one from afar. Be open-minded and try to take the best route for you.

Think of this book as you might about fashion, creating your own combinations to suit personal tastes and preferences. There are really several recipes within each dish—dozens of sauces, garnishes, fillings, bases, and other elements. Each of these can be used as part of a meal, as an addition to a salad or dessert, or in any number of ways. My best suggestion is to read this book in its entirety, cover to cover, and get familiar with it, just like you might your own wardrobe. Think of it and all of its elements as part of your culinary arsenal and make use of it accordingly. Most of dishes in this book are structured as they would be in a restaurant environment or at an important event or celebration. Still, the basic elements and techniques of the book are all applicable on a regular basis, and can be used in the same way that much simpler recipes might be. Ideally, as a reader of the book, you will feel that your possibilities for raw food preparation have been expanded.

Every meal is a unique experience and, therefore, a recipe is simply a tool to help enhance that experience. While I have suggested how to present my recipes with photographs and assembly instructions, you may prefer to serve everything family style. Tacos, for example, would be great with the components in separate bowls and the naked shells available for everyone to choose from. Let guests fill them, make them part of that experience, and it usually works out well. I may use a garnish that you don't have access to—it's only a garnish, but changing a green, or removing spice here and there, will not seriously compromise a dish. You will often have leftover sauces or fillings. Some recipes are easier to produce in larger quantities and don't work well in very small batches due to equipment limitations or other reasons. That said, I've never seen an extra cup or two of chocolate sauce, marshmallow cream, or raw ice cream go to waste. In fact, it may just be good for breakfast.

Just remember, it's about the experience, not only with what's on the plate, but how you arrived at the plate. If you've enjoyed it to that stage, you'll have a great meal.

if nothing ever changed,
there'd be no butterflies.

—Tom Robbins, *Still Life with Woodpecker*

blossom

Every spring, I encounter a moment where I am transported back to my childhood during an unseasonably warm afternoon on the coast of Maine. It is really a sensation of earthy aroma: the warming sun combined with thawing soil, as if the light is melting away winter. Like no other place, Maine embraces each season with abandon and teaches its inhabitants not to hold on for too long, but to savor it while it lasts. When I first began my journey as a chef, I lacked many of the tools that some of my colleagues had: a tradition of a family with a deeply rooted culinary background, lifelong access to specialty markets and restaurants, growing up as a gourmand. In fact, Searsport, Maine, is far better known for its quaint coastal charm than for any of its culinary aptitude. Still, I was fortunate to have a childhood that taught me more about seasonality than all of my future years of cooking combined.

In the summer, I could walk across the street from my home to the edge of the field in front of Penobscot Bay and pick tiny, sweet wild strawberries, blackberries, and raspberries directly from their vines. My grandfather's cherry tree provided sweet fruit for eating, with pits to launch at my cousins. My dad would navigate our way across a fast-flowing river onto his "mountain," where we would forage fiddlehead ferns in the wild. We always had a garden, and the memories are secure in my mind . . . taste of earth, aroma of sun, crisp, watery, and colorful—husking corn, shelling peas, even the rattling cover of my mom's cookware as the water heated to cook the summer vegetables.

As time has passed, my appreciation for seasonal produce has only expanded. As a chef, I learned to become excited about autumn mushrooms, the first early asparagus and green garlic, even the cool of winter when citrus fruits and root vegetables provide a new culinary challenge . . . beets and orange zest, with a little pistachio oil and sea salt . . . it all makes sense and is the way we should be eating.

With raw food, the emphasis on seasonality is even more important. There is no smoky grill to mask the essence of the ingredients, no deep-frying that really strips rather than adds flavor. This is naked cuisine—presented in its purest form, creatively combined, but with its character always retained. A cook has nothing greater to celebrate than the seasons.

In time, a seasoned chef will expend the same effort—perhaps more—in sourcing ingredients as in preparing them. If I were to make a Moroccan tagine for dinner on a fall evening in New York, it could mean biking to the Greenmarket for autumn squash and pumpkin, visiting Sahadi's (my favorite Middle Eastern market) for pomegranates and almonds, crossing the bridge to Kalustyan's for spices, and on it goes. No amount of diligence will ever be too much.

Cherry and apple blossoms on their branches, baskets of brown pears, sugar pumpkins, crab apples, and fresh wildflowers are only a fraction of what is available for us when setting a table or creating a room that evokes seasonality. The same influences that guide our menu choices provide elegant nuances to luscious cocktails and cool beverages. I am so enamored with seasonality, embracing each one with such passion, that the onset of longer days and brighter sun, the cool crisp breeze of an approaching winter, or the quiet lazy days of summer are each worthy of throwing a long lunch, a dinner, or a cocktail party. We may as well enjoy them before they pass. And just as you become enamored with those beautiful heirloom tomatoes, they will disappear.

sweet pea flan with macadamia foam, lime powder, and black sesame tuile

When my team and I first plated it, I experienced the rush that accompanies an intense creative effort that ends in success. The colors are remarkable, and it is every bit as silky and smooth as a flan should be. It is one of my most highly recommended dishes for a dinner party that includes many guests who are new to raw.

FLAN
3 cups cashews, soaked 1–2 hours
$1/2$ cup coconut meat
$1/4$ cup prepared Irish moss
$1/4$ cup juice of sugar snap peas
$1/2$ teaspoon salt
8 large fresh mint leaves

FOAM
1 cup macadamia nuts, soaked 1–2 hours
3 cups water
Salt
Soy lecithin

LIME POWDER
1 pint lime zest

TUILE
$1/4$ cup ground black sesame seeds
$1/2$ cup flax meal
$1/2$ cup chopped yellow squash
1 tablespoon lemon juice
1 cup water
1 tablespoon raw agave
$1/2$ teaspoon salt
$1/4$ teaspoon coriander seeds
$1/2$ teaspoon ground cumin

FLAN Blend all ingredients in a Vita-Mix until very smooth. Pour into lightly oiled flan or custard ramekins and place in the refrigerator for at least 1 hour, until firm.

FOAM Blend all ingredients in Vita-Mix until smooth; strain through a chinois and reserve.

LIME POWDER Spread zest on Teflex sheets and cover with a dehydrator screen. Dehydrate overnight until completely dry. Place in Vita-Mix and blend into a powder.

TUILE Place ground sesame seeds in a large bowl; set aside. Blend remaining ingredients in Vita-Mix until smooth.

Combine mixture with the sesame seeds. Spread over Teflex sheets in a very thin layer. Dehydrate 6–8 hours until dry but still very pliable. Cut into long thin triangles. Arrange each over cylinder shapes, such as a rolling pin, on dehydrator trays; dehydrate until crisp.

ASSEMBLY Use a small offset spatula to loosen sides of flan and turn out onto a serving dish. Place a tuile near the flan. Blend macadamia foam, 2–3 cups at a time, in Vita-Mix. Spoon foam from top of mixture and drizzle close to flan, hugging the edges, for garnish. Sprinkle with lime powder. SERVES 4–6

cream of matsutake soup, pignoli dumplings, pears, and tarragon

The matsutake is highly valued by the Japanese—and for good reason. It is said to be an aphrodisiac and has a wonderful nutty, spicy flavor. Matsutake, also known as the pine mushroom, grow under pine trees that are between twenty and sixty years old, and never in the same place twice. These mushrooms are said to be high in vitamins and low in calories, and are thought to prevent aging. Most of all, I love their taste. This recipe is my favorite of all the raw soups I have had—it is extremely decadent, elegant, and refined, a wonderfully earthy and filling dish.

FILLING
1 cup pine nuts, soaked 1–2 hours
1 tablespoon lemon juice
$1/2$ teaspoon salt
1 teaspoon nutritional yeast
2 tablespoons scallions

DUMPLINGS
2 cups coconut meat
$1/4$ cup spinach juice
$1/4$ teaspoon sea salt
1 bunch chives

SOUP
About 20 matsutake mushrooms, cut from stem, divided
Salt
Olive oil
2 cups pine nuts, soaked 1–2 hours
6 cups water
$1/4$ cup white miso
1 tablespoon chopped fresh tarragon
2 tablespoons soy lecithin
Black pepper

GARNISH
1 pear, cut into matchsticks
Olive oil
Black pepper
Fresh tarragon leaves

FILLING Process all ingredients in a food processor until smooth.

DUMPLINGS Blend all ingredients except chives in a Vita-Mix until smooth. Spread thin on Teflex sheets. Dehydrate 4–5 hours until dry but still very flexible. Trim edges and cut into 9 squares per sheet. Place small amount of filling in center of wrapper; pull up edges around cheese and form a beggar's purse. Tie to secure with a chive.

SOUP Toss mushrooms with salt and enough olive oil to lightly coat them. Blend pine nuts, water, salt, miso, tarragon, and soy lecithin until smooth. Strain through a chinois. Spread on Teflex sheets; dehydrate 1–2 hours. Blend $3/4$ of the mushrooms with the puréed ingredients and reserve the remainder for garnish. Season with salt and black pepper to taste.

ASSEMBLY Pour the soup in deep bowls. Float two dumplings in the center, garnishing around it with pear matchsticks. Drizzle with a touch of olive oil, top with freshly cracked black pepper, and garnish with tarragon leaves and remaining mushrooms. SERVES 4

basil black pepper wrappers, macadamia "cheese," cherry tomatoes, and avocado

The discovery of using young coconut as a wrapper and all-purpose replacement for pasta and rice paper was a miracle for us at my former restaurant the Plant. We have since evolved to using it in many forms, colors, and flavors, with this dish being one of my favorites. Often the best dishes are those that are somehow familiar to us, and I don't know anyone who doesn't like tomato and basil together. These are also great for entertaining because the components can be made in advance and assembled by the guests or just before serving. They're addictively delicious.

WRAPPERS
4 cups coconut meat
1/4 cup spinach juice
1 cup fresh basil leaves
1/4 teaspoon salt
1/2 teaspoon coarsely ground black pepper

"CHEESE"
2 cups macadamia nuts, soaked 1–2 hours
2 tablespoons lemon juice
1 tablespoon nutritional yeast

1/2 medium-size shallot
3/4 teaspoon salt

DRIED CHERRY TOMATOES
1 cup halved ripe cherry tomatoes
Olive oil
Pinch salt

GARNISH
Basil leaves
1 avocado, halved, pitted, and thinly sliced

WRAPPERS Blend all ingredients except black pepper until very smooth. Spread very thin on Teflex sheets, sprinkle with the black pepper, and dehydrate 3–4 hours. Remove from Teflex and trim edges. Cut in 9 squares and reserve. They hold best when placed between wax paper and kept cool.

"CHEESE" Process all ingredients in a food processor until well combined. Crumble mixture onto dehydrator screens and dehydrate 4–6 hours. Store in refrigerator.

DRIED CHERRY TOMATOES Toss the cherry tomatoes with olive oil and salt, and spread on dehydrator screens. Dehydrate 3–4 hours. Remove and set aside at room temperature.

ASSEMBLY Place the wrappers flat on a work surface. Put 1 teaspoon "cheese" in the center of each wrapper and top with avocado, cherry tomatoes, and a fresh basil leaf. Lightly wet two of the opposite corners with a touch of water and roll them from one side, with the corner just reaching over the filling. Roll the other corner over that, forming a boat shape. Press tightly so they remain together.
SERVES 4–6

squash blossoms with pistachio purée, green zebra fondue, pine nuts, and purple basil

For a raw chef, summer means outdoor farmers markets, and also food with tremendous vibrancy and color that can be easier to prepare than more elaborate winter dishes. Everyone generally thinks of squash blossoms as a dish that is stuffed (sometimes with cheese, crab, or pork), battered, and fried. Admittedly, they can be delicious in their traditional form, but they are also just as tasty raw and are a great carrier for other summer flavors—this dish combines so many of my favorite ingredients that I can easily make a meal from it. The green zebra fondue was an experiment that rewarded me with a new way to make sauces, and is one that I'll use over and over again.

SQUASH BLOSSOMS
24 stemmed and cleaned squash blossoms (carefully clean and wash blossoms, leaving less than 1 inch of stem)

PURÉE
3 cups pistachios, soaked 1–2 hours
1/4 cup lemon juice
1/2 cup water
1/2 cup olive oil
2 1/2 teaspoons salt

2 teaspoons nutritional yeast
2 tablespoons raw agave

FONDUE
1/4 cup olive oil
3 cups chopped green zebra tomatoes
Salt and pepper to taste
1/4 cup julienned basil

GARNISH
1 1/4 cups roughly chopped pine nuts
Purple basil leaves

PURÉE Process ingredients in a food processor 3–5 minutes until smooth.

FONDUE Toss olive oil and tomatoes together in a bowl. Place bowl in a dehydrator for 1–2 hours. Blend all ingredients in a Vita-Mix until very smooth, season with salt and pepper, and stir in basil.

ASSEMBLY Stuff the squash blossoms with purée until plump. Divide the fondue and place on the bottom of each plate. Top each with 6 squash blossoms. Garnish with chopped pine nuts and purple basil. SERVES 4

ginger cantaloupe "gelato" and watermelon granité with muscat honeydew purée

Back in the day when I used to be a frequent restaurant patron, I would go to great lengths to dine at New York's best restaurants. The original Bouley in Tribeca was a phenomenal place, with food and décor that were always magical. David Bouley, the chef and owner, offered each guest a special dish after main courses, just before dessert. It was light melon soup with some of the lightest sorbets I have ever had. The combination of two soft cool textures together is something I never forgot—this dish is inspired by that.

"GELATO"
1/2 cup cashews, soaked 1–2 hours
1 cup macadamia nuts, soaked 1–2 hours
1/4 cup coconut meat
3/4 cup raw agave
2 1/2 cups cantaloupe juice
1/4 cup ginger juice
2 teaspoons vanilla extract
Pinch sea salt
1/4 cup coconut oil

GRANITÉ
1 medium-size ripe watermelon
1/4 cup raw agave

PURÉE
1/2 cup semisweet white wine, preferably Riesling
1 honeydew melon, seeded and blended
1/4 cup raw agave
1 vanilla bean, scraped
1/4 teaspoon salt

GARNISH
Fresh mint leaves, lavender sprigs, or edible flowers

"GELATO" Blend all ingredients in a Vita-Mix until smooth. Pour into an ice cream maker and freeze according to manufacturer's directions.

GRANITÉ Mash watermelon through a medium chinois. Add agave and freeze in a shallow pan. Allow the top to begin to freeze, about 2 hours, then lightly mash with a fork. Continue this every couple of hours until the mixture is frozen and flaky.

PURÉE Blend all ingredients in Vita-Mix until very smooth.

ASSEMBLY Place two scoops of "gelato" and one scoop of granité in each of four bowls. Pour enough honeydew purée into each bowl to reach halfway up the sides of the "gelato." Float a few mint leaves or flowers in the purée for garnish. SERVES 4–6

frozen chocolate pudding with cinnamon-glazed plums, chocolate basil wafers, and vanilla bean–plum syrup

I dare anyone not to like chocolate and plums. Is that even possible? It seems that everyone loves chocolate these days. I like to combine it with seasonal fruits, particularly stone fruits, which provide a good balance with their tartness and also a slightly nontraditional pairing.

PUDDING
2 cups cashews, soaked 1–2 hours
2 cups coconut meat
1 cup water
1^1/$_4$ cups raw agave
1 cup coconut oil
1 teaspoon vanilla extract
^{1}/$_2$ teaspoon sea salt
1^1/$_4$ cups cacao powder
2 tablespoons raw carob powder

PLUMS
1 cup raw agave
3 tablespoons ginger juice
2 teaspoons ground cinnamon
^{1}/$_2$ teaspoon ground star anise
Pinch salt
8 plums, various sizes and colors if possible, halved, pitted, and cut into eighths

WAFERS
2^1/$_2$ cups cashew flour
1^3/$_4$ cups oat flour
1^1/$_2$ teaspoons sea salt
^{1}/$_4$ cup water
1 cup maple syrup
1 cup cocoa powder
^{1}/$_2$ cup packed fresh basil leaves
1 tablespoon vanilla extract

SYRUP
1 cup raw agave
1^1/$_2$ cups pitted and chopped sugar plums
^{1}/$_4$ teaspoon salt
1 vanilla bean, scraped
2 tablespoons vanilla extract

GARNISH
Fresh mint sprigs

PUDDING Blend all ingredients in a Vita-Mix until completely smooth. Pour into a half sheet or low-sided baking dish and chill in freezer until firm.

PLUMS Blend all ingredients except plums in Vita-Mix until smooth. Toss with plums in a shallow baking dish and set aside at room temperature.

WAFERS Mix flours and sea salt in a medium-size bowl. Blend the remaining ingredients in Vita-Mix until smooth. Add to flour mixture and mix well with hands. Spread very thin long rectangles on Teflex sheets and dehydrate 6 hours. Turn onto screens and dehydrate until crisp, another 8–12 hours.

SYRUP Blend until smooth in Vita-Mix. Strain through a fine chinois.

ASSEMBLY Place a 3-inch ring mold in the center of a plate and scoop enough chocolate pudding into it until 2 inches high. Press top with a spoon to pack it and smooth the top. Remove ring carefully. Top with a pile of plums (they should be naturally piled on top; if some are falling, that is fine). Spoon generous amounts of the plum syrup around the plate and garnish with mint sprigs and wafers. SERVES 4–6

marinated tomato salad, pine nut "parmesan," basil oil, micro greens, and black pepper

Farmers markets embody summer, and New York now has a very passionate audience that patronizes them. The Union Square Greenmarket may be the most well known, but when I was living in Brooklyn, I began to visit the one in Park Slope, on the edge of Prospect Park. It is not the largest in the city, but it is quite substantial and the products are amazing. It was there that I found some of the most beautiful tomatoes of my life, bursting with color, with flavor so intense that you could almost taste the sun inside each bite. I also purchased several varieties of basil for the best tomato salad I've ever had.

TOMATOES
1/4 cup olive oil
2 tablespoons raw agave
Salt
Black pepper
1 1/2 pounds halved red, yellow, and green cherry
   tomatoes

"PARMESAN"
2 cups pine nuts
1/2 cup water

1 teaspoon olive oil
1 tablespoon sea salt
2 tablespoons lemon juice
2 tablespoons nutritional yeast

OIL
1 bunch fresh basil leaves
1 cup pure olive oil

GARNISH
Fresh basil sprigs
Salt and pepper

TOMATOES Mix all ingredients together.

"PARMESAN" Process all ingredients in a food processor until well combined. Spread in 1/8-inch-thick slices on Teflex sheets in a dehydrator and heat until it becomes firm, about 12 hours. Turn over Parmesan sheets onto dehydrator screens and continue dehydrating for 24 hours. Remove, let cool, and break into 2- or 3-inch shards. Keep covered.

OIL Place basil leaves in a blender with the olive oil. Purée until smooth. Place in a bowl or low-sided pan and put into dehydrator for 30 minutes. Strain through a fine-mesh strainer into a sterilized airtight jar or bottle. This will keep in a cool dark place for up to 1 week.

ASSEMBLY Arrange the cherry tomatoes on plates, with most having the center of the tomato facing up. The presentation should be natural—just quickly pour them on the plates and turn over a few that are facing down. Drizzle with basil oil, sprinkle with salt and pepper, and garnish with basil leaves and "Parmesan" shards. SERVES 4

golden tomato and lemon cucumber gazpacho with avocado salsa

Gazpacho is one of my favorite summer meals—I love not only the texture and flavor contrasts but also the ease of preparation. On a beautiful warm evening, I'm often in the mood for something that can be quickly prepared. With a blender and some really fresh ingredients, this dish can be made in five minutes. Gazpacho is best served chilled, with an equally cool glass of white wine.

GAZPACHO

2 cups peeled, deseeded, and diced lemon cucumbers
2 cups deseeded and diced tomatillos
$2^1/4$ cups diced golden tomatoes
2 tablespoons lime juice
$1/2$ jalapeño pepper
Salt to taste
2 tablespoons olive oil

AVOCADO SALSA

1 avocado, diced
1 tablespoon chopped cilantro
1 teaspoon minced jalapeño
1 teaspoon lime juice
Salt and pepper to taste

GARNISH

Olive oil
Black pepper

GAZPACHO Mix all ingredients except olive oil in a large bowl; season to taste. Place $3/4$ of mixture in a food processor and process until smooth. Add back to bowl and stir to combine.

AVOCADO SALSA Combine all ingredients.

ASSEMBLY Serve chilled with avocado salsa, a few drops of olive oil, and freshly ground pepper. SERVES 4

apricots with star anise syrup and crumble

With raw food, as with all cooking, we often make things as complex as possible before we simplify them. In my early days with this food, I was always searching for a magical pastry recipe for desserts; but these days, especially in the summer, I like to focus on retaining the fruits' natural texture and flavor while subtly enhancing it. This dish could not be simpler to prepare and is easily adapted to peaches, nectarines, or any other stone fruit.

Apricots were first discovered growing in the wild on mountainsides in China and were brought to California by the Spanish, where 95 percent of the U.S. apricots are now grown. Although our harvest on the East Coast is limited, for the few weeks we have apricots, they are delicious and abundant at farmers markets.

APRICOTS
16 apricots
$3/4$ cup raw agave

CRUMBLE
$2^1/2$ cups cashew flour
$1^1/4$ cups oat flour
6 tablespoons water

$3/4$ cup plus 2 tablespoons maple syrup
1 tablespoon vanilla extract
$1^1/2$ teaspoons sea salt
1 tablespoon cinnamon

SYRUP
1 cup raw agave
$1/2$ teaspoon ground star anise
2 tablespoons lemon juice

APRICOTS Cut apricots in half and discard stones. Toss fruit with agave. Place on dehydrator screens and dehydrate 20–30 minutes.

CRUMBLE Mix ingredients in a medium-size bowl by hand. Spread flat on dehydrator screens. Dehydrate 8–10 hours until dry; crumble by hand and place back in dehydrator.

Dehydrate overnight. Process in a food processor into crumbs.

SYRUP Blend ingredients in a Vita-Mix to combine.

ASSEMBLY Place 8 apricot halves on each plate. Sprinkle top with crumbs just before serving. Spoon syrup over each serving. SERVES 4

beet ravioli with fava bean purée and green herb oil

When most people think of a beet, they are considering the standard red beet—there is nothing wrong with that, or the phrase "beet red," but I love beets for their versatility in the same way that I love tomatoes and plums for their many varieties, tastes, and textures. In the summer, when golden, white, red, candy stripe, and other varieties are available directly from the garden, they are good in many raw food preparations. Given that root vegetables are rather fibrous, they are best when sliced thin, minced, or otherwise broken down in such a way to easily consume—and they also taste better this way. I like using them as a carpaccio or, in this recipe, preparing them like a carpaccio and using them as the outside of a ravioli. The day I prepared this dish, it was late August in Maine and fava beans were still in season. With a little olive oil, they were lightly warmed, making a very sweet, nutty purée that was a good counterbalance to the crunch of beet, not to mention a very colorful combination.

BEETS
10 medium-size varietal beets (candy stripe, white, golden, red)
$1/4$ cup olive oil
3 tablespoons lime juice
1 tablespoon raw agave

PURÉE
$1^1/2$ pounds shelled fava beans
$1/4$ cup olive oil
2 tablespoons lemon juice
$1/2$ teaspoon salt

2 tablespoons chopped fresh mint
1 tablespoon nutritional yeast
2 tablespoons chopped fresh basil

OIL
1 cup fresh green herb leaves (mint, basil, oregano, parsley)
1 cup pure olive oil

GARNISH
Fresh summer herbs

BEETS Peel the beets and trim the edges to make them square. Slice very thin on a mandolin, keeping each type of beet separate. Combine the remaining ingredients and lightly brush the beet slices.

PURÉE Peel and rinse fava beans. Combine with olive oil and warm in a dehydrator for 90 minutes. Process until smooth with remaining ingredients.

OIL Place herb leaves in a blender with the olive oil. Purée until smooth. Place in a bowl or low-sided pan and put into dehydrator for 30 minutes. Strain through a fine-mesh strainer into a sterilized airtight jar or bottle. This will keep in a cool dark place for up to 1 week.

ASSEMBLY Prepare a "sandwich" of the beets by placing 1 tablespoon fava purée on $1/2$ of the slices. Top with the other slice and lightly press together, but not so much that the purée comes past the sides. On each plate, place 1 of each type of "ravioli," and on each plate, at least one duplicate. There should be 5–6 on each plate. Drizzle with herb oil and garnish with fresh herbs. SERVES 4

plum carpaccio with vanilla-agave syrup and ginger cream

This carpaccio may be the prettiest dish I have ever worked with. One day, I came back from the Greenmarket with the most beautiful plums but had no idea what to do with them; it soon became apparent that I needed to keep them as whole as possible. I made a quick vanilla syrup with agave and sliced the plums thin enough to have a bit of translucency to them but thick enough to have a little crunch.

CARPACCIO
4 red plums
4 yellow plums
4 blue plums
4 purple plums

SYRUP
1 cup raw agave
1 vanilla bean, scraped

CREAM
1 cup cashews, soaked 1–2 hours
$1/2$ cup water
2 tablespoons ginger juice
1 tablespoon raw agave
Pinch sea salt

GARNISH
Lavender sprigs

SYRUP Combine ingredients and mix well.

CREAM Blend all ingredients in a Vita-Mix until smooth. Keep cool.

ASSEMBLY Wash the plums, halve them, remove pits, and slice very thin using a mandolin or sharp knife. Place the plum slices on each plate, alternating the colors. Just before serving, pour enough syrup over just to coat. This dish is going to take you 10 minutes to make. Slicing the plums close to when they are being served is recommended. Garnish with a scoop of cream and lavender sprigs.
SERVES 4

raspberry parfait, vanilla bean cream, dark chocolate sauce, and coconut brittle

Some dishes are simply crowd-pleasers, combining a number of components and ingredients that have mass appeal. I love inventive combinations and textures, but I must admit, if I could eat one dessert only, it might be this. It's easy to love and easy to adapt to different fruits, flavored creams, and any number of crunch additions such as spiced macadamia nuts, candied almonds, or whatever you desire.

BRITTLE
- 1 cup dried coconut
- 1 cup macadamia nuts, dehydrated overnight and chopped
- $1/3$ cup maple syrup powder
- $1/4$ cup maple syrup
- 1 tablespoon ground ginger

CREAM
- 2 cups young coconut meat
- $1/4$ cup raw agave
- $1/2$ vanilla bean, scraped
- 2 tablespoons lemon juice
- 2 tablespoons melted coconut oil
- $1/4$ teaspoon sea salt

SAUCE
- $1^1/2$ cups cacao nibs
- $1^1/4$ cups raw agave
- $1/2$ cup coconut oil
- 1 cup maple syrup
- 1 tablespoon vanilla extract
- Pinch sea salt

GARNISH
- 1 quart raspberries
- Fresh mint leaves, optional

BRITTLE Process all ingredients in a food processor just until combined. Spread into a thin, uneven layer on Teflex dehydrator sheets and dehydrate 8–10 hours. Turn onto screens and dehydrate overnight. Break apart into small pieces and dehydrate another 6–8 hours.

CREAM Blend all ingredients in a Vita-Mix until completely smooth. Chill before serving.

SAUCE Blend all ingredients in Vita-Mix until completely smooth.

ASSEMBLY Warm chocolate sauce slightly in dehydrator. Place about $1/2$ inch of chocolate sauce at the bottom of a martini or stemmed cocktail glass. Add a layer of raspberries, then a layer of cream, sprinkle with brittle, and repeat until there are three layers of each. Finish with a final layer of chocolate. Top the parfait with raspberries and mint leaves. SERVES 4

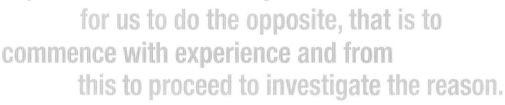

Although nature commences
with reason and ends in
experience it is necessary
for us to do the opposite, that is to
commence with experience and from
this to proceed to investigate the reason.

—Leonardo Da Vinci

contemporary

You've probably already guessed that contemporary would be my favorite chapter. What most interests me about food is the relationship between time, history, experience—and taste. The spatial differences are profound in some cases, and I was fortunate to learn this early in my career. On a trip to Morocco many years ago, I was taken to a very traditional restaurant in the Medina of Marrakesh, a place where time seems to have stopped and the narrow streets are paved with history and tradition. Upon entering Yacout through a massive old wooden door, you are transported into a magical world of sensory feelings: the feeling of warmth, the smell of spice, the glow of lanterns, the silence of greenery, and the pull of seduction placed on all diners. It is, for the most part, indescribable; but many, including me, will try to convey the experience in words.

It was there that I first tasted the famous Moroccan Lemon Chicken, which is known for its distinct flavor of salty preserved lemon, green olives, and ginger. The chicken was cooked like a stew, with bones, and in a sauce rich with onion, saffron, ginger, and hot pepper. It is a haunting flavor that one can never forget. I left Morocco after that visit with an eagerness that I will always seek to replenish—the desire to be in a kitchen and apply my own set of culinary skills—armed with my newly acquired taste memories.

Back in New York, one of the city's most esteemed chefs, Jean-Georges Vongrichten, was in the process of opening his first restaurant as an owner, called JoJo, on Manhattan's Upper East Side. Jean-Georges is known for his wildly inventive use of infused oils and juices, all rooted in traditional cooking, and I was very excited to try his new restaurant. I was there on opening night and dozens of times in the next two years. On one of my early visits, I ordered a dish simply described as Chicken (with olives, lemon, and chickpea fries). It sounded simple enough and looked very light and clean—a very contemporary presentation like many other New York dishes at the time. And then, one bite, the flavors exploded, and I was taken back to Yacout—but this was New York. What was happening? I discovered, eventually, what more seasoned chefs already had. Flavors, feelings, moods, and ideas were transportable. The higher-end chefs were not simply cooks; they were artists, inspired by real-life experience and emotion. In the beginning, as in any art, it appears that replication may be taking place, but the reality is that inspiration may appear in a variety of forms. In this case, it was clear that Jean-Georges had probably shared a similar experience to mine and applied that to his own brand of cuisine. He found an avenue to reapply experience—in this case, taste memory—into his art.

With raw food, outside influences are very important. With a short history of culinary imagination, the cuisine is still in its infancy. In order for it to reach its highest potential, it is necessary to connect with individuals on an emotional and physical level, and then, on a more basic note, as a chef. I'd like to point out that the preparation of raw food is so new that I can't think of a better canvas for creative food.

When I initially became involved in raw food, my early influences were traditional dishes that were well known: lasagna, ravioli, pasta, and so forth. Over the past couple of years, my style has evolved well beyond that, and I now find that the most interesting cuisine is based on life—or art that represents life experience. Whether it is film, sculpture, architecture, or music, I believe that the path to the highest level of this cuisine is through its relationship to art; and for that reason, much of my food is influenced by it. The best dishes have come from this concept—the inspiration may be the Rolling Stones, Salvador Dali, or *The Wizard of Oz*. The importance of a connection to deeper meaning is paramount. Often, the concept is simpler, such as a black-and-white dinner that I once did: foods that were black and white and nothing more. The important element is to push the boundaries, find the core, and, ultimately, provide a great experience for guests.

black-and-white tofu, trumpet mushroom salad, sesame enoki mushrooms, white asparagus, and miso broth

Often, in the pursuit of art, I purposely work within concepts that apply narrow limitations. The results, like the movements of a contortionist, are always interesting. The purpose of this exploration is not solely to be creative or different but to better understand the possibilities within the cuisine. The black-and-white menu was one of the most challenging menus I've done, and I learned a great deal from it, including how to prepare this tasty and dramatic recipe.

WHITE TOFU
1 cup cashews, soaked 1–2 hours
$1/2$ cup fresh young Thai coconut meat
$1/2$ cup raw carageenan
$1/2$ cup water
$1/4$ teaspoon sea salt

BLACK TOFU
1 cup cashews, soaked 1–2 hours
$1/2$ cup fresh young Thai coconut meat
$1/2$ cup raw carrageenan
$1/4$ cup water
$1/4$ cup ground black sesame paste
$1/4$ teaspoon sea salt

MUSHROOMS
1 cup enoki mushrooms
2 tablespoons sesame oil
1 teaspoon nama shoyu
Pinch sea salt

SALAD
1 cup black trumpet mushrooms
1 tablespoon white miso
1 teaspoon minced fresh ginger
1 tablespoon sesame oil
1 tablespoon lemon juice
1 tablespoon raw agave

ASPARAGUS
1 small bunch asparagus
2 tablespoons olive oil
Pinch salt

BROTH
1 cup water
$1/2$ cup nama shoyu
2 tablespoons dried dulse
1 tablespoon wakame
$1/4$ cup miso paste

WHITE TOFU Line the bottom and sides of a small pan or square container with plastic wrap. Drain cashews. Blend all ingredients in a Vita-Mix until completely smooth. Pour into lined pan, then cover with plastic wrap. (Tofu should be about $1\frac{1}{2}$ inches thick.) Refrigerate about 2 hours until firm. When ready to serve, remove tofu from container by lifting plastic wrap out of pan and gently transferring tofu to a cutting board. Cut tofu into 2-inch squares with a butter knife. Repeat this same procedure for black tofu.

MUSHROOMS Combine all ingredients and allow mushrooms to marinate for at least 1 hour.

SALAD Toss mushrooms with remaining ingredients; spread on Teflex sheets and dehydrate 20–30 minutes.

ASPARAGUS Cut white asparagus into 1-inch lengths on a bias and toss just to coat with olive oil and season with salt; dehydrate 45 minutes.

BROTH Combine all ingredients. Place in a dehydrator for 90 minutes. Strain and reserve.

ASSEMBLY On a large, preferably high-rimmed plate, set two pieces of tofu, one of each color (the plates can alternate which have two of each). Garnish the white tofu with salad; garnish the black tofu with mushrooms. Pour enough broth into each bowl to come up to $1/4$ of the tofu's height and place a few asparagus spears inside the broth.
SERVES 4

black sesame and white coconut dumplings with creamy miso sauce

These dumplings are perhaps the most stunning dish I have ever served—they are ultra simple and elegant, like a black-tie affair, but the concept is undeniably charming and sophisticated. Fortunately, they taste even better than they look and have became an instant classic of mine.

BLACK SESAME DUMPLINGS
2 cups young coconut meat
^{1}/3 cup black sesame tahini
^{1}/4 teaspoon salt

WHITE COCONUT DUMPLINGS
2 cups young coconut meat
^{1}/4 teaspoon salt

FILLING
4 cups cashews, soaked 1–2 hours
4 tablespoons sesame oil
2 teaspoons salt
4 tablespoons nama shoyu
4 tablespoons minced scallions
4 tablespoons minced fresh ginger

MISO SAUCE
^{1}/2 cup cashews, soaked 1–2 hours
^{1}/3 cup tahini
^{1}/4 cup white miso
^{1}/4 cup nama shoyu
^{1}/4 cup packed dulse
^{1}/4 cup raw agave
^{1}/4 cup ginger juice

GARNISH
Chives
2 tablespoons chopped scallions
^{1}/4 cup black sesame tahini

BLACK SESAME DUMPLINGS Blend ingredients in a Vita-Mix until smooth. Spread very thin on dehydrator Teflex sheets and dehydrate 3–4 hours. Remove from Teflex and invert onto a cutting board. Trim edges evenly. Cut into 9 squares. Repeat this same procedure for the white coconut dumplings.

FILLING In a food processor, pulse the cashews until coarsely minced. In a separate bowl, combine cashews with remaining ingredients.

MISO SAUCE Blend all ingredients in Vita-Mix until smooth.

ASSEMBLY To prepare the wrappers, brush one side of the white wrapper with water and lay a black wrapper across it diagonally so that there are 8 points. Brush with water and place 1 tablespoon filling in the center. Pull the outsides together so that the dumplings bunch together like a sack. Tie a chive around each to secure.

On each plate, pour 3 tablespoons sauce in the center and spread gently with a spoon, being careful not to let sauce go to the edges of the plate. Place 2 dumplings on each plate, and drop just a few drops of black sesame tahini on the plate. YIELDS 16

jackson pollock raviolo with arugula pesto

I've rarely had such a good time plating a dish as I did this raviolo. The coconut wrappers have become so versatile in my repertoire that the "pasta" itself was easy, especially having so many great fruit and vegetable juices to work with. But the real fun was "splattering" the plates (and the floors and clothes) with the pesto. Although this is a very serious and advanced dish, in its own subtle way, the concept of letting loose a little is a nice reminder that food preparation need not be rigid and limited. In fact, taking risks and expanding our methods will often lead to intriguing results.

It doesn't make much difference how the paint is put on as long as something has been said. Technique is just a means of arriving at a statement. —*Jackson Pollock*

RAVIOLO

WRAPPERS
4 cups young Thai coconut
1 teaspoon salt
$1/4$ cup frozen mango purée
$1/4$ cup blended and strained red pepper purée
$1/4$ cup spinach juice

FiLLING
$3^1/2$ cups Brazil nuts, soaked 2–3 hours
$1/4$ cup fresh lemon juice
$1/2$ cup water

1 cup olive oil
$1^1/2$ teaspoons salt
2 teaspoons nutritional yeast

PESTO
2 cups packed arugula
1 cup packed mint
1 cup packed parsley
$1/4$ cup pine nuts
1 teaspoon salt
Black pepper
$1/2$ cup olive oil

WRAPPERS Blend coconut and salt in a Vita-Mix until very smooth. Spread thin on Teflex dehydrator sheets and dehydrate 1 hour. Pull out sheets and splatter coconut wrappers with purées and spinach juice. Dehydrate another $2^1/2$ to 3 hours. Remove colored sheets from Teflex, trim edges, and cut into 6 rectangular pieces.

FILLING Process all ingredients in a food processor 3–5 minutes until smooth.

PESTO Process all ingredients except olive oil in food processor until combined and chunky. With machine running, add olive oil. Check seasoning.

ASSEMBLY Place 1 tablespoon raviolo filling just off center of each pasta sheet—fold over to make corners meet, press edges together, and flatten a bit by hand. Place two raviolo on each plate and splatter plate with pesto. SERVES 4–6

shiitake ravioli with broccoli rabe, balsamic fig purée, and ginger cream

Around the time I began working with raw foods, I was also practicing a lot of yoga, about two hours each day in the early afternoon. As I grew more comfortable in my postures, my mind began to expand; and after the sessions, I did my best thinking. I was pressed for a new dish for a potential magazine article about what I was working on and, with very little practical experience with this cuisine, a variation of this dish appeared in my imagination. In execution, it was exactly as I had envisioned, along with a substantial amount of extra labor that I did not plan for. The concept is one that can be applied to many different dishes—simply by changing the vegetable or modifying the sauce with different spices. For example, a bok choy, sesame, and ginger filling with a curry cream would be excellent.

WRAPPERS
4 young Thai coconuts

FILLING AND RABE
2 cups shiitake mushrooms, quartered
$1/4$ cup olive oil, divided
Salt
Pepper
2 cups broccoli rabe, cut into 2-inch lengths

PURÉE
6 dried figs
1 cup balsamic vinegar
2 tablespoons raw agave nectar
$1/4$ teaspoon ground anise seed

CREAM
1 cup cashews, soaked 1–2 hours
1 cup reserved coconut water
3 tablespoons ginger juice
1 tablespoon raw agave
Sea salt

WRAPPERS Open coconuts; strain water and reserve. Chop top off coconut, just where it begins to turn inward. Carefully remove the coconut meat using the back of a spoon, keeping the bottom in 1 piece and the top in 1 piece. Cut coconut into 2-inch squares, and then, very carefully, slice each in half the long way, making several very thin pasta squares.

FILLING AND RABE Toss mushrooms in a bowl with half the olive oil, and season with salt and pepper. Spread on Teflex sheets and dehydrate 45 minutes. Toss the broccoli rabe with remaining olive oil, season with salt and pepper, and dehydrate 1 hour.

PURÉE Blend all ingredients in a Vita-Mix until smooth.

CREAM Blend all ingredients in Vita-Mix until smooth.

ASSEMBLY Dip each pasta square in the ginger cream and place 4 on each plate. Add broccoli rabe and $2/3$ of the mushrooms to top each square. Top with another pasta square, then remaining mushrooms. Drizzle sauce around raviolis and fig sauce over the tops. SERVES 4

green tea canneloni, banana lemongrass cream, almond "gelato," and goji lime sauce

One of my earliest experiments was a Japanese dinner, where we pushed the boundaries with a number of new dishes. I recall writing the menu and wondering how in the world we would actually make this dish. Kristen, one of the sous chefs, did an amazing job by fulfilling the vision and creating one of the most sophisticated desserts to come out of my kitchen.

CANNELONI
2^1/$_2$ cups oat flour
1^1/$_2$ cups cashew flour
^{1}/$_4$ teaspoon salt
2 tablespoons raw agave
^{1}/$_2$ teaspoon vanilla extract
^{1}/$_2$ cup maple syrup
2^1/$_2$ tablespoons green tea powder

CREAM
1^1/$_2$ cups cashews, soaked 1–2 hours
1^1/$_2$ ripe bananas
^{1}/$_2$ cup coconut meat
^{1}/$_4$ cup lemongrass juice
^{1}/$_2$ teaspoon salt
1 vanilla bean, scraped
1 tablespoon fresh lemon juice
2 tablespoons water
^{1}/$_4$ cup raw agave
^{1}/$_4$ cup coconut oil

"GELATO"
^{1}/$_2$ cup cashews, soaked 1–2 hours
1 cup macadamia nuts, soaked 1–2 hours
^{1}/$_4$ cup coconut meat
^{3}/$_4$ cup raw agave
1 cup water
2 teaspoons vanilla extract
1 tablespoon almond extract
Pinch sea salt
^{1}/$_2$ cup coconut oil

LIME SAUCE
^{1}/$_4$ cup goji berries, soaked 15 minutes and strained
^{1}/$_4$ cup raw agave
^{1}/$_2$ cup lime juice
1 tablespoon lime zest

CANNELONI Using your hands, mix ingredients until well combined. Roll thin and cut with a ring mold; wrap around a cylinder to shape canneloni. Dehydrate 48 hours.

CREAM Blend all ingredients in a Vita-Mix until smooth.

"GELATO" Blend all ingredients in Vita-Mix until smooth.

LIME SAUCE Blend all ingredients in Vita-Mix until smooth.

ASSEMBLY Fill each canneloni with cream. Place a pool of lime sauce on each plate and set canneloni on sauce. Scoop "gelato" close to canneloni. SERVES 4

ocean vegetables and squash noodles with oyster-mushroom escabeche, faded green caviar, and miso tahini sauce

Sea vegetables are simply incredible—the flavors are all unique, as are the textures—and they harbor some of the most important nutrients we ever need. For a vegan, it becomes even more important to find tasty sources of these minerals, and these are the best. Now that they have become mainstream, it is quite possible to build elaborate flavors and presentations around them.

VEGETABLES
4 ounces pink seaweed (tosaka), washed and soaked overnight
4 ounces wakame, reconstituted
4 ounces hijiki, reconstituted
4 ounces kelp, reconstituted
4 ounces light green seaweed (ogonori), washed and soaked overnight
4 ounces arame, reconstituted
Black and white sesame seeds
1 small knob fresh ginger, cut into very thin batons
1 medium beet, cut into very thin batons
1 small carrot, cut into very thin batons
1 small zucchini, cut into thin spirals
1 small jicama, peeled and cut into very thin batons

NOODLES
1 yellow squash, cut into long noodles with a spiralizer
Salt
Olive oil

ESCABECHE
$1/2$ cup olive oil

$1/4$ cup apple cider vinegar
1 teaspoon ground mustard
1 tablespoon dried oregano
1 teaspoon salt
1 teaspoon black pepper
8 ounces oyster mushrooms

CAVIAR
6 ounces arame
$1/2$ cup Irish moss
$1/4$ cup water
3 tablespoons spinach juice
Pinch salt

SAUCE
$1^1/2$ cups raw agave
2 cups tahini
$1^1/2$ cups water
$1^1/4$ cups miso
$1/4$ cup lemon juice

GARNISH
Black and white sesame seeds

NOODLES Toss pasta with a bit of salt and olive oil. Form pasta into spiral bunches on Teflex sheets and dehydrate overnight. Transfer to a screen if needed and place another screen over spirals to keep in place; dehydrate an additional 24 hours.

ESCABECHE Blend all ingredients except mushrooms in a Vita-Mix and pour into a bowl. Add mushrooms, let marinate 15 minutes, then dehydrate on Teflex sheets for 20 minutes.

CAVIAR Soak the arame in warm water for 1 hour and drain. Blend all ingredients until very smooth and spread 1 inch thick onto a loaf pan. Refrigerate 4 hours. With the end of a small espresso spoon, lift out a very small (pearl-size) amount of the caviar. Spread these pearls onto a flat plate or pan.

SAUCE Blend ingredients in Vita-Mix.

ASSEMBLY Dress each of the sea vegetables separately with sauce. Dress each of the raw vegetables also with the sauce. Prepare individual large tablespoon-size piles of each sea vegetable in a serpent shape, with a different raw vegetable topped on each one. Alternate sprinkling them with black and white sesame seeds. On the arame, top with faded green caviar, and on the wakame, top with the crisp squash noodles. SERVES 4

gnocchi of broccoli rabe with ginger cream sauce, concord grape chutney, manchego paper, and dust of three leaves

The most alluring aspect of the New York Greenmarket in fall is the presence of Concord grapes—and their amazing juice—that a couple of farmers sell in Union Square. Bitter, sweet, salty, and sour are four sensations that, when properly combined, create the highest possible form of flavor. Broccoli rabe and Concord grapes really should be a classic combination!

BROCCOLI RABE GNOCCHI
1 cup chopped broccoli rabe
3 tablespoons olive oil
$1/2$ teaspoon salt
$1/4$ teaspoon black pepper
4 cups jicama, processed in food processor until finely pulsed and strained of excess water
2 cups cashews, soaked 1–2 hours
$1^1/2$ teaspoons sea salt
1 teaspoon nutritional yeast
$3/4$ cup fresh lemon juice
$1/2$ cup cashew flour

CHUTNEY
2 cups Concord grapes
2 cups seedless red grapes, diced small
1 teaspoon lime juice
Pinch freshly ground pepper
1 tablespoon minced ginger

SAUCE
1 cup cashews, soaked 1–2 hours
$3/4$ cup water
3 tablespoons ginger juice
2 tablespoons raw agave
$1/2$ teaspoon salt

MANCHEGO PAPER
4 cups coconut meat
$1/2$ teaspoon salt
3 tablespoons nutritional yeast
1 teaspoon fresh lemon juice

DUST OF THREE LEAVES
20 basil leaves
20 mint leaves
30 parsley leaves

BROCCOLI RABE GNOCCHI Marinate broccoli rabe in olive oil, salt, and pepper, then dehydrate 30 minutes.

Mix jicama, cashews, sea salt, nutritional yeast, lemon juice, and black pepper to taste in a large bowl. Blend in batches in a Vita-Mix until very smooth. Place all ingredients in a bowl and stir in cashew flour. Chop marinated and dehydrated broccoli rabe and gently stir into mixture by hand. Shape mixture into gnocchi and gently roll on screens to create a gnocchi pattern. Place in dehydrator for 2 hours until crust forms around outside. Serve immediately, or warm in dehydrator until ready to serve.

CHUTNEY Crush the Concord grapes through a strainer and reserve juice. In a food processor, pulse the grape juice, lime juice, pepper, ginger, and red grapes to combine, just a few seconds, but not to fully purée. Dehydrate in a shallow pan for 2 hours and let cool.

SAUCE Blend all ingredients in Vita-Mix until smooth.

MANCHEGO PAPER Blend all ingredients in Vita-Mix until completely smooth. Spread in a thin layer over dehydrator Teflex sheets. Dehydrate 4–5 hours, then break into large sheets.

DUST OF THREE LEAVES To make basil dust, place basil leaves between dehydrator screens. Dehydrate overnight or until crisp. Run through Vita-Mix to make into powder. Repeat process separately with mint and parsley leaves.

ASSEMBLY Sauce the gnocchi with enough ginger cream to lightly coat it. On one side, garnish with the grape chutney. Lay the manchego paper across the top and make three lines of herb dust across the top of that. SERVES 4

frozen pumpkin flan, cinnamon foam, and mandarin candy

Whenever I think of pumpkin, I can't help but remember the image of myself in a giant papier-mâché pumpkin that my dad made for me on Halloween many years ago. Ever since, it's been a lighthearted association. Interestingly enough, this dish is actually made with carrot, which provides the same starchiness, and the pumpkin spices supply the rest.

FLAN

FILLING

3 cups cashews, soaked 2–3 hours
$1/2$ cup maple syrup
$1/2$ cup raw agave
1 cup coconut oil
$1^1/4$ cups carrot juice
1 teaspoon vanilla
$1/2$ teaspoon salt
$1/4$ vanilla bean, scraped
3 teaspoons ground cinnamon
3 teaspoons ground nutmeg

CRUST

$2^1/2$ cups cashew flour
$1^3/4$ cups oat flour
$1/4$ cup water
$3/4$ cup maple syrup

1 tablespoon vanilla
$1^1/2$ teaspoons sea salt
1 tablespoon ground cinnamon
2 teaspoons ground nutmeg

FOAM

$1^1/2$ cups cashews, soaked 1–2 hours
3 cups water
2 teaspoons ground cinnamon
$1/4$ cup raw agave
$1/4$ cup coconut oil
1 vanilla bean, scraped

CANDY

3 cups coconut meat
1 cup fresh orange juice
$1/2$ teaspoon salt
$1/4$ cup maple syrup
$1/2$ cup orange zest

FILLING Blend all ingredients in a Vita-Mix until very smooth. Pour into plastic-lined ramekins and freeze.

CRUST Mix ingredients in a medium-size bowl by hand. Spread flat on dehydrator screens. Dehydrate at 115 degrees F for 4–5 hours until dry; crumble onto Teflex sheets. Dehydrate an additional 5 hours.

FOAM Blend cashews and water in Vita-Mix until smooth; strain through a fine chinois. Return cashew milk to Vita-Mix with remaining ingredients; blend until smooth. Use an immersion blender to create foam.

CANDY Blend all ingredients except zest in Vita-Mix until completely smooth. Spread in a $1/8$-inch-thick layer over dehydrator Teflex sheets and sprinkle zest over top. Dehydrate 4–5 hours, cut into strips, and carefully wrap around cylinders. Dehydrate until crisp.

ASSEMBLY Using a square or round ring mold, press $1/4$ inch of the crust into the bottom of the mold and top with the flan. Remove mold and drizzle foam around edges. Top with mandarin candy. SERVES 4

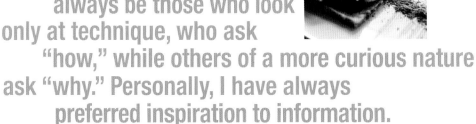

Of course, there will
    always be those who look
only at technique, who ask
    "how," while others of a more curious nature
ask "why." Personally, I have always
    preferred inspiration to information.

—Man Ray

inspiration

If food were simply about nourishment, life would be far less exciting. Instead, we are blessed with magical ingredients and recipes that offer us everything from a sense of euphoria to improved sleep to increased sex drive. I like to call these characteristics "inspirational" in honor of their ability to add to our life experiences in one way or another. Whether it is for a special symbolic occasion or simply everyday living, food contributes to the quality of our lives in both subtle and more potent ways.

History helps us here: generations pass down remedies, cures, and unique perspectives on certain foods. Tradition offers much in the way of putting reason behind certain preparations, and our own sensitivity, perhaps most importantly, directs our own choices. I know, for example, that raw cacao gives me energy, enlivens my palate, and creates positive thinking when I really need a boost. I'm quite confident that a cold, ripe red grapefruit will give me a buzz in the morning and that sweet peas in summer will always bring back memories.

This is also the age of superfoods—in part due to our society's hunger for a quick fix, but also because there are many more talented global foragers introducing products to the marketplace than ever before and more consumers taking notice of the wonders of certain foods. In the raw world, people are especially diligent in their perseverance and ability to communicate the benefits of these foods to the larger public. The results are more products available on the market and more creative people finding ways to use them.

Regardless of the cause of our inspiration, the ability of great food to enrich our lives through health, memory, or any positive form of stimulation remains one of life's great rewards.

white corn tamale, serrano-spiced portobello, raw cacao mole, and guacamole

Occasionally, the unusual taste of cacao fits perfectly with a savory dish—and this mole is an example of that. Rather than an unnecessary sweetness, it is nutty, deep, earthy, and, of course, very, very spicy. A few bites will wake up any palate in no time.

TAMALE
5 cups white corn kernels, divided
2 medium tomatoes, seeded and minced
1 red bell pepper, seeded and minced
$1/4$ cup chopped sun-dried tomatoes
$1 1/4$ cups pine nuts, soaked 1–2 hours
$1 1/4$ cups cashews, soaked 1–2 hours
1 teaspoon sea salt
$3/4$ teaspoon nutritional yeast
2 tablespoons minced red onion
2 tablespoons chopped fresh cilantro
1 clove garlic, peeled and minced
$3/4$ cup fresh lime juice

PORTOBELLO
4 portobello mushrooms, cut in half and into 8 slices
    per side
3 tablespoons olive oil
1 serrano chile, seeded and minced
Salt and freshly ground black pepper

MOLE
6 dried ancho/chipotle chiles, soaked 2–3 hours and
    drained
$1/2$ cup chopped red onion
2 cloves garlic, minced
2 tablespoons sunflower seeds, soaked 4–6 hours and
    drained

$1/2$ cup almond butter
$1/2$ cup raisins, soaked 20–30 minutes
6 tablespoons olive oil
1 cup water
2 tablespoons raw agave
2 teaspoons ground cumin
$1/2$ teaspoon ground coriander
1 teaspoon salt
$1/4$ teaspoon cayenne
1 cup cacao powder

CORNHUSKS
Soak 6 cornhusks in warm water for 1–2 hours

GUACAMOLE
3 ripe avocados, peeled, pitted, and roughly chopped
1 large handful cilantro leaves, finely chopped
2 tablespoons fresh lime juice
1 teaspoon sea salt
$1/2$ scallion, finely chopped
$1/2$ red chile, finely minced
1 jalapeño, seeded and minced

GARNISH
Cacao powder
Cilantro leaves

TAMALE Place $1 1/2$ cups corn, the tomatoes, and the bell pepper in a bowl; set aside. In a food processor, blend the remaining ingredients until very smooth. Pour into bowl with other ingredients and mix well with hands.

PORTOBELLO Toss mushrooms with olive oil, serrano, salt, and pepper, then spread on Teflex sheets to dehydrate for 12–24 hours. Mix corn filling with portobello or reserve and serve on the side with tamales.

MOLE Blend all ingredients in a Vita-Mix until smooth.

CORNHUSKS Dry the cornhusks carefully. Lay cornhusks flat and place about $1/2$ cup corn mixture onto the center of each. Fold the bottom up over the filling and then fold the sides over. Using the husk strips, tie the tops of each tamale. Place the tamales in dehydrator for 2 hours.

GUACAMOLE Place all ingredients in a small bowl and mash well with a fork.

ASSEMBLY Spoon a generous amount of mole sauce on each plate, and set 2 tamales on sauce. Spoon Guacamole on top and garnish with cacao powder and cilantro leaves. SERVES 4–6

bitter broccoli ravioli and pine nut "cheese" in chocolate wrappers with orange powder and pinot noir sauce

One of the main dishes from a cacao dinner I hosted, this dish features ravioli where the "pasta" are made from cacao—it is one of the most straightforward preparations I have offered but so powerful and to the point that less is more. It has all of the elements—bitter, salty, sour, and sweet—that combine to create a complex harmony of flavor.

"CHEESE"
1 cup pine nuts, soaked 1–2 hours
2 tablespoons fresh lemon juice
$1/4$ teaspoon salt
$1/2$ teaspoon nutritional yeast
$1/2$ scallion

RABE
2 cups roughly chopped broccoli rabe
Juice of 1 lemon
3 tablespoons olive oil
$1/4$ teaspoon salt
$1/4$ teaspoon black pepper

WRAPPERS
2 cups young coconut meat
4 tablespoons raw cacao powder
$1/4$ teaspoon salt

SAUCE
2 cups Pinot Noir
$1/2$ cup pomegranate juice
1 tablespoon black peppercorns
1 small sprig rosemary
$1/4$ cup dried cherries
Juice of 1 lemon

POWDER
1 cup orange zest

"CHEESE" Process all ingredients in a food processor until smooth.

RABE Toss all ingredients in a large bowl. Spread on Teflex sheets and dehydrate 30 minutes.

WRAPPERS Blend all ingredients in a Vita-Mix until very smooth. Spread mixture in a thin even layer over a Teflex sheet and dehydrate 3 hours. Store in plastic wrap in refrigerator until ready to use. Remove from refrigerator and allow the mixture to adjust to room temperature prior to use. Trim edges and cut into 16 squares.

SAUCE In a shallow pan, dehydrate Pinot Noir, pomegranate juice, black peppercorns, and rosemary until liquid has reduced by 50 percent, about 8 hours. Strain liquid and blend with remaining ingredients.

POWDER Spread zest on Teflex sheets and cover with a dehydrator screen. Dehydrate overnight until completely dry. Blend in Vita-Mix into a powder.

ASSEMBLY Mix broccoli rabe into "cheese" for the filling. To prepare the ravioli, place a teaspoon of filling just off center on each square and fold over, pressing each together softly. Line the raviolis in a row on plates and drizzle with sauce; garnish with orange powder. **SERVES 4**

chocolate chili tacos with marinated arugula, pear tomatoes, and pignoli "sour cream"

Cacao, the raw cocao bean—not to be confused with processed or sweetened chocolate—is quickly becoming the most well-known superfood in the raw world. It is an excellent source of magnesium and ananamide, which is known as the "bliss chemical," bringing on a sense of well-being. It is a stimulant and, although slightly pungent, its unique taste is pleasant, especially in a recipe like this.

TACO SHELLS
3 cups fresh corn
$1^1/2$ cups chopped red bell pepper
$3/4$ cup flax meal
$1/2$ cup water
1 tablespoon fresh lime juice
$1^1/2$ teaspoons chili powder
$1^1/2$ teaspoons sea salt
2 teaspoons cumin
2 tablespoons raw cocoa powder

"SOUR CREAM"
2 cups pine nuts, soaked 1–2 hours
1 cup water
$1/2$ cup olive oil
3 tablespoons fresh lemon juice
1 teaspoon sea salt

ARUGULA
1 quart fresh arugula, packed and gently torn
Olive oil
Sea salt
Black pepper

TOMATOES
1 pint pear tomatoes, halved
3 tablespoons olive oil
$1/2$ teaspoon salt
Black pepper
$1/4$ cup julienned basil

GARNISH
1 avocado, optional
10 basil leaves, coarsely chopped, optional

TACO SHELLS Blend all ingredients in a Vita-Mix until smooth. Spread on Teflex sheets to ¼-inch thickness in 5- or 6-inch rounds; dehydrate at 118 degrees F for 3–4 hours; flip and dehydrate 30 minutes more. Fold in half to shape into taco shells; dehydrate overnight.

"SOUR CREAM" Blend all ingredients in Vita-Mix until completely smooth. Pour into quart containers.

ARUGULA Toss arugula with enough olive oil to lightly coat, then add sea salt and black pepper to taste. Place arugula in a bowl and cover with plastic wrap; let sit in a dehydrator at 118 degrees F for 15–20 minutes, until wilted.

TOMATOES Toss tomatoes with olive oil, salt, and pepper; dehydrate 3 hours. Add basil.

ASSEMBLY Divide the arugula among the taco shells; add pear tomatoes and a generous amount of "sour cream." Top with avocado and fresh basil. SERVES 4–6

cinnamon graham cookie with marshmallow crème and dark chocolate fondue

Admittedly, this is a raw version of s'mores—I had been talking about making this dish for many weeks when I needed a chocolate dessert for a contemporary menu we had been planning. It is comfort food in disguise and a potent version at that.

COOKIE
5 cups cashew flour
2^1/$_2$ cups oat flour
^{3}/$_4$ cup water
1^3/$_4$ cups maple syrup
2 tablespoons vanilla extract
1 tablespoon sea salt
2 tablespoons cinnamon

CRÈME
2 cups cashews, soaked 1–2 hours
1 cup coconut meat
1 tablespoon vanilla extract
^{1}/$_2$ teaspoon salt

^{1}/$_2$ cup raw agave
^{1}/$_4$ cup coconut oil
1 small (1.25-ounce) bottle Lorann Marshmallow Concentrated Oil

FONDUE
4 cups maple syrup
2^1/$_2$ cups raw cocoa powder
2 cups coconut oil
1 teaspoon vanilla extract
^{1}/$_2$ teaspoon salt

GARNISH
2 tablespoons cinnamon

COOKIE Mix ingredients in a medium-size bowl by hand. Spread flat to ^{1}/$_8$ inch thick on dehydrator screens. Dehydrate at 115 degrees F for 4 hours. Make an incision with the back of a knife for six rectangles. Dehydrate another 6 hours, then separate pieces. Keep well sealed, at room temperature, until ready to serve.

CRÈME Blend all ingredients in a Vita-Mix until smooth. Pour into a plastic-lined half sheet pan; refrigerate overnight or freeze 1–2 hours prior to serving.

FONDUE Whisk all ingredients in a large bowl. Blend in batches in Vita-Mix. Pour into half sheet pan and store in freezer.

ASSEMBLY Bring crème to room temperature at least 20 minutes prior to serving. Warm chocolate and cookies slightly in dehydrator. Place 1 cookie on a plate. Carefully spread a generous amount of crème on top and pour an even more generous amount of fondue over that, allowing it to slightly run off onto the plate. Set another cookie on top, but off center, exposing the crème and fondue. Sprinkle the plate with cinnamon. SERVES 4

cacao crêpes and sweet mint custard with black cacao sauce

When I was first experimenting with raw cacao, it was challenging to use—it was not yet available in powder form, and the taste was unusual, so I was a bit unsure of it—but the dried beans actually reacted well to certain recipes, especially those where a soft texture is needed. This dish is pure classic in flavor.

CRÊPES
1 quart flax meal
1 quart apples, peeled, cored, and chopped
2 cups chopped coconut meat
2 cups cocoa powder
$1/4$ cup fresh lemon juice
2 quarts water
2 tablespoons maple syrup
$1/4$ cup raw agave
$2^1/4$ teaspoons salt

MINT CUSTARD
2 cups cashews, soaked 4–6 hours
1 cup coconut meat
1 tablespoon vanilla extract
$1/2$ teaspoon salt
$1/2$ cup raw agave
$1/4$ cup coconut oil
$3/4$ teaspoon peppermint oil

JAM
1 pint raspberries
$1/4$ cup Irish moss
$1/4$ cup raw agave
1 tablespoon lemon zest

SAUCE
$2^1/2$ cups raw agave
1 cup cocoa powder
$1/4$ cup carob powder
$1/2$ teaspoon vanilla
$1/4$ teaspoon salt
$1/4$ cup maple syrup
$1^1/4$ cups coconut oil

BANANA "ICE CREAM"
1 cup cashews, soaked 1–2 hours
$1/2$ cup coconut meat
$1/2$ cup raw agave
$1^1/4$ cups water
2 fresh bananas, peeled
1 teaspoon lemon juice
$1/4$ vanilla bean, scraped
Pinch sea salt
$1/2$ cup coconut oil

CRÊPES Blend all ingredients in a Vita-Mix. Spread thinly into 4- or 5-inch rounds on dehydrator Teflex sheets (9 per tray). Dehydrate 5–6 hours, or until dry but very pliable.

MINT CUSTARD Blend ingredients in Vita-Mix until smooth. Place in quart containers and freeze. Run in a Pacojet, freeze, and then run again. Makes 1 quart.

JAM Blend all ingredients in a food processor, chill for 3 hours.

SAUCE Blend ingredients in Vita-Mix until smooth.

BANANA "ICE CREAM" Blend all ingredients in Vita-Mix until very smooth. Pour into an ice cream maker and follow manufacturer's instructions.

ASSEMBLY Fill the crêpes with mint custard and jam. Scoop banana "ice cream" to the side and pour chocolate sauce over top. SERVES 4–6

frozen mint panna cotta with marshmallow whip, vanilla wafers, and bittersweet cacao sauce

This requires marshmallow extract, but if it is unavailable, extra vanilla bean will be fine. As with many desserts, the components of this will work well with any number of recipes.

PANNA COTTA
3 cups cashews, soaked 1–2 hours
$1/2$ cup coconut meat
$1^1/2$ cups raw agave
2 cups water
4 teaspoons vanilla extract
$1^1/2$ teaspoons nonalcoholic peppermint extract
$1/4$ teaspoon sea salt
1 cup coconut oil
6 tablespoons spinach juice
$2/3$ cup chopped pistachios
$1/2$ cup cacao nibs

WHIP
$1^1/2$ cups cashews, soaked 1–2 hours
$1^1/2$ cups coconut meat
1 cup raw agave nectar
$3/4$ cup extra-virgin coconut oil
$1/4$ cup water
2 teaspoons vanilla extract
$1/2$ teaspoon sea salt
1–2 bottles marshmallow extract

WAFERS
3 cups fine cashew flour
$1^3/4$ cups almond flour
$1/4$ cup coconut oil
1 cup maple syrup
4 teaspoons vanilla extract
4 vanilla beans, scraped
$1^1/2$ teaspoons sea salt
Lemon juice
1/2 teaspoon cinnamon

SAUCE
3 cups raw agave
$1^1/2$ cups raw cacao powder
$1/4$ cup raw carob powder
$1/2$ teaspoon vanilla extract
$1/4$ teaspoon sea salt
$1/2$ cup coconut oil

PANNA COTTA Blend all ingredients except pistachios and cacao in a Vita-Mix until smooth. Stir in pistachios and nibs. Freeze in custard molds until ready to use.

WHIP Blend all ingredients in Vita-Mix until very smooth. Chill in freezer 3–4 hours, then whip in a blender.

WAFERS Mix ingredients in a medium-size bowl by hand. Spread to $1/8$ inch thick on Teflex sheets and dehydrate 4–5 hours. Cut into desired shapes and place on dehydrator screens; dehydrate an additional 4–5 hours.

SAUCE Blend ingredients in Vita-Mix until smooth.

ASSEMBLY Unmold panna cotta onto plates—garnish with whip and drizzle sauce over the top. Stick two wafers into each panna cotta. SERVES 4–6

oreo cookie with cream filling, vanilla bean "ice cream," and black cocoa syrup

This is chocolate and vanilla, simply presented in a new form. I swore off my youthful penchant for junk food many years ago, but Kristen, a very talented chef I worked with, tempts me with these recipes and I feel that I am regressing.

COOKIE
4 cups raw cocoa powder
4 cups oat flour
$1^1/_2$ teaspoons Himalayan salt
1 cup maple syrup
1 cup raw agave
3 tablespoons coconut oil, melted
$1^1/_2$ teaspoons vanilla extract

CREAM FILLING
3 cups cashews, soaked
1 cup coconut meat
1 tablespoon vanilla extract
$1/_2$ teaspoon salt
$1/_2$ cup raw agave
$3/_4$ cup coconut oil

"ICE CREAM"
$1^1/_2$ cups cashews, soaked 1–2 hours
$1/_2$ cup coconut meat

$1/_2$ vanilla bean, scraped
$1/_4$ teaspoon sea salt
$1/_4$ cup raw agave
$1/_4$ cup plus 2 tablespoons coconut oil

SYRUP
$2^1/_2$ cups raw agave
1 cup cocoa powder
$1/_4$ cup carob powder
$1/_2$ teaspoon vanilla
$1/_4$ teaspoon salt
$1/_4$ cup maple syrup
$1^1/_4$ cups coconut oil

GARNISH
Fresh black peppermint

COOKIE Mix together dry ingredients in a large bowl. Add remaining ingredients to dry ingredients. Mix well with hands. Line a 9 x 13-inch pan with parchment paper. Press into pan in an even layer and dehydrate overnight. Flip onto a cutting board, cut into circles with a ring mold or cookie cutter, and place on dehydrator screens and dehydrate another 4–6 hours.

CREAM FILLING Blend all ingredients until smooth in a Vita-Mix. Pour into a plastic-lined half sheet pan; refrigerate overnight or freeze 1–2 hours prior to serving.

"ICE CREAM" Blend all ingredients until smooth in Vita-Mix. Process in an ice cream maker and freeze.

SYRUP Blend all ingredients in Vita-Mix until smooth.

ASSEMBLY Fill cookies with cream filling (like Oreos). Serve with chocolate sauce and "ice cream," and garnish with peppermint. SERVES 10–12

"...we get to think of life as an inexhaustible well. Yet everything happens only a certain number of times, and a very small number, really.... How many more times will you watch the full moon rise? Perhaps twenty. And yet it all seems limitless."

—Paul Bowles

spice

The best expression, whether through food, literature, art, or film, often takes us on a journey to a place either new or forgotten. Transporting is the word often referenced when a meal not only excites our senses but also removes us from the present and places us into the captivating and unknown. I know of no other cuisine that is more sensual and deeply rooted in history and mystery as that which makes ample use of spices. There are many factors that contribute to this.

Spices have been an important economic commodity throughout history and have had a major impact on exploration, trade, and travel. They are beloved by many nations for the exotic flavors they lend to cooking, as well as for their many therapeutic and medicinal properties. I was first captivated by spices during an extended trip to Morocco, where the outdoor markets offered enormous baskets of them—filled with the deepest hues of oranges, reds, yellows, and ochres—like a glowing sunset.

Over the years, I have been introduced to dishes from around the world—most of my favorites have a powerful yet refined use of spices, from coriander to saffron to my favorite, white cardamom. These flavors and colors not only have influenced my cooking and palate but also have given me "taste memories" that will stay with me forever. I am remembering the first vegetable tagine I had in Fez so many years ago—it is as distinct as if I first tried it this morning and yet is so far away.

Spices must be used in moderation and respected for their inherent character. They must always be fresh and well stored, preferably whole or recently ground. Utilize them as you might a photo album or a brief vacation—let them transport you to another land and place far away, or let them bring you home again.

heirloom tomato pavé and preserved lemon dressing with green olives and pine nuts

I'll never forget the day I returned from a two-week trip to Morocco, filled with ideas and taste memories. I could not wait to get into the kitchen at my original restaurant, Matthew's, to experiment with what I had learned and with some of the ingredient combinations that I had been thinking about. It was this first Moroccan trip where I found my footing as a chef and began to learn how to "reinterpret" food in a way that it would remain grounded and focused but also take on its own originality. In Morocco, I had tasted an amazing lemon chicken with olives, preserved lemon, pine nuts, and saffron. My version of "lemon chicken" remained on my menu for many years, and though I haven't had chicken or poultry in years, the memory is of the nutty, sweet-and-sour lemon flavor. I try to incorporate it into food whenever I can. This dish was a big success at my restaurant The Plant and is relatively easy to make as long as you have good, ripe, firm tomatoes.

PAVÉ
4 large golden, green, or red tomatoes, peeled and cored

DRESSING
$1/4$ cup preserved lemons
2 tablespoons fresh lemon juice
$1/4$ cup almond oil
2 tablespoons raw agave nectar

3 tablespoons pitted green olives
Salt
Pepper
Water

GARNISH
Pine nuts
$1/4$ cup julienned preserved lemon peel
Cilantro leaves

PAVÉ Slice tomatoes thinly lengthwise by running a sharp knife parallel to flat surface. Trim into squares.

DRESSING Process all ingredients in a food processor. Add water to thin if necessary.

ASSEMBLY Brush a small amount of dressing on tomato slices to coat lightly. Overlap them in a long row or a large square. Drizzle with more sauce, sprinkle with pine nuts and preserved lemon slices, and garnish with cilantro leaves. SERVES 4

shiitake bisteeya with ginger-cilantro sauce,
candied almonds, and wilted spinach

I credit my ability to be creative with raw food to the exotic foods I experimented with over many years as a traditional chef and as a consumer of pretty much any food that was available throughout the world. The first time I saw a bisteeya, it was awe-inspiring. Standing in the courtyard of a private palace in Morocco, I saw the chefs carrying silver trays with the giant crackling, sugar-coated, savory pies known as bisteeya. These were filled with chicken, pigeon, almonds, sugar, egg, and spices—and were utterly delicious. In fact, on a food tour of Morocco, I visited a cooking school outside of Rabat, which specialized in teaching the preparation of Warka, the pastry specifically made for this dish. The school was mesmerizing—for its silence and also for the fact that it was only available to women.

To serve Bisteeya implies a celebration of sorts, and that is what we had in mind for our Moroccan Friday at The Plant with this raw version. I can't claim that it is as crispy as the original version, but it is quite tasty, nonetheless.

BISTEEYA WRAPPERS
Recipe coconut wrappers (see page 76)

BISTEEYA MUSHROOMS
1 cup thinly sliced shiitake mushrooms
2 tablespoons olive oil
Salt
Black pepper

CANDIED ALMONDS
6 cups almonds
$1/3$ cup plus 1 tablespoon maple syrup
1 teaspoon vanilla extract
$1/2$ tablespoon sea salt
$1^1/2$ tablespoons ground cinnamon
$1^1/2$ cups maple powder

SAUCE
$1/4$ cup minced ginger
$1/4$ cup almonds, soaked 4 hours

1 cup water
2 tablespoons raw agave
$1/4$ cup cilantro leaves
Salt

SPINACH
1 cup young spinach leaves
1 tablespoon olive oil
1 teaspoon fresh lemon juice
$1/2$ teaspoon lemon zest
Salt and pepper

GARNISH
$1/4$ cup cilantro leaves
1 teaspoon cinnamon
1 teaspoon turmeric

BISTEEYA MUSHROOMS Toss shiitake slices with olive oil, salt, and pepper, then dehydrate on Teflex sheets for 30–60 minutes.

CANDIED ALMONDS Soak nuts overnight; drain. Dehydrate 24 hours. In a large bowl, coat dehydrated nuts with maple syrup. Combine vanilla, salt, cinnamon, and maple powder, and stir into nuts until they are well coated. Dehydrate on screens for 48 hours.

SAUCE Blend all ingredients in a Vita-Mix until smooth.

SPINACH Combine all ingredients and dehydrate 20 minutes.

ASSEMBLY Mix mushrooms with candied nuts, cilantro leaves, and enough sauce to bind them together.

Cut each sheet of wrappers into 3 strips, and cut those in half. Place a dollop of filling at the near end of wrapper and fold over, corner to corner, to make triangle shapes.

Scatter spinach on plates, top with bisteeya, and garnish with cinnamon and turmeric. **SERVES 4**

avocado tartare with tamarind-glazed cherry tomatoes, black sesame pappadam, and curry froth

Raw food fans typically love avocados, and for good reason. They evoke fun, sensuality, richness, and nutrition, and are extremely versatile in food preparation. The idea of doing this dish as a tartare was to awaken our guests' palates with an exotic, but not overpowering, starter during the spice dinner. Although there are many potentially powerful elements to this, they are used in a subtle manner and in such a way that the goal of teasing and awakening the taste buds was successful.

TARTARE
2 ripe avocados, diced
2 tablespoons lime juice
1 teaspoon lime zest
2 tablespoons macadamia nut oil
Salt
Black pepper
2 tablespoons chopped cilantro
1 teaspoon crushed coriander seed
1 jalapeño, minced

PAPPADAM
1 cup flax meal
1 cup chopped yellow squash
$1/2$ cup chopped coconut meat
1 tablespoon fresh lemon juice
2 cups water
2 tablespoons raw agave
$1/2$ teaspoon salt
$1/2$ teaspoon coriander
$1/2$ teaspoon cumin
$1/4$ cup black sesame seeds

FROTH
$1^1/2$ cups red bell pepper, puréed
2 cups chopped mango
$3/4$ teaspoon salt
2 tablespoons curry powder
$1/2$ teaspoon garam masala
$1/4$ teaspoon paprika
$1/4$ teaspoon turmeric
$1/2$ cup cashews, soaked 1–2 hours
2 tablespoons fresh lime juice
3 tablespoons sesame oil
1 teaspoon nama shoyu

TAMARIND-GLAZED CHERRY TOMATOES
$1/2$ cup halved cherry tomatoes
1 cup dried tamarind, soaked 30 minutes
$1/4$ cup raw agave
1 teaspoon chili powder
1 teaspoon cayenne
2 tablespoons fresh lime juice
2 tablespoons sesame oil

TARTARE Gently mix all ingredients in a medium bowl. Line soufflé cups with plastic wrap and gently press mixture into cups. Refrigerate 1–2 hours. Unmold directly onto serving dish.

PAPPADAM Blend all ingredients except sesame seeds in a Vita-Mix until smooth. Spread thinly into 3-inch rounds on dehydrator Teflex sheets; sprinkle with black sesame seeds. Dehydrate 5–6 hours, flip, and dehydrate until crisp.

FROTH Blend all ingredients in Vita-Mix until smooth.

TAMARIND-GLAZED CHERRY TOMATOES Dehydrate tomatoes until soft, about 1 hour. Remove seeds from tamarind, push pulp through a coarse strainer, and blend in Vita-Mix with remaining ingredients. When ready to assemble, toss tomatoes with enough tamarind glaze to coat them.

ASSEMBLY Invert tartare on plates and top with tomatoes. Blend froth to create foam and spoon a generous amount of foam around each tartare. Garnish with pappadam.
SERVES 4–6

sweet pea samosas, mint-almond chutney, and pickled lime "yogurt"

My childhood fondness for sweet flavors was ultimately balanced with the introduction of sour, via my experience with Mediterranean, and particularly Sicilian, cooking. *Agrodolce*, which in Italian translates to "sweet and sour," is a great concept, and when used properly, adds a surprise element to food. In this recipe, the sweetness of the peas and the coconut wrapper of the samosas is nicely balanced with the pickled lime yogurt. This is one of my favorite dishes ever to come out of my former restaurant The Plant.

WRAPPERS
2 cups chopped coconut meat
Pinch sea salt
$1/2$ cup chopped mint leaves

FILLING
1 cup chopped jicama
2 cups raw sweet peas
1 cup macadamia nuts
$1/2$ cup water
1 teaspoon coriander
1 teaspoon garam masala
1 teaspoon chili powder
1 teaspoon salt
Black pepper to taste
2 tablespoons nutritional yeast
2 tablespoons chopped cilantro
1 tablespoon chopped mint

CHUTNEY
$1^1/2$ cups almonds, soaked 8–10 hours
$1^1/4$ cups fresh mint, roughly chopped
$1/4$ cup orange zest
$1/4$ cup fresh lemon juice
$1/4$ cup raw agave
1 teaspoon chili powder
1 cup olive oil
1 teaspoon salt
Black pepper

"YOGURT"
$1^1/2$ cups cashews, soaked 1–2 hours
1 cup coconut meat
$1/2$ cup water
$1/3$ cup fresh lime juice
Zest of 3 limes
$1/2$ teaspoon salt

GARNISH
Mint leaves

WRAPPERS Blend coconut and salt in a Vita-Mix until very smooth; stir in mint. Spread mixture in a thin layer over 2 dehydrator teflex sheets for 4–5 hours until fully dehydrated. Remove wrappers from sheets, trim edges, and cut into 4 even strips. Store in plastic wrap until ready to use.

FILLING Process jicama in a food processor until well minced. Add peas to gently crush. Set aside. In a Vita-Mix, blend macadamia nuts, water, spices, salt, pepper, and nutritional yeast. Add to pea mixture and check seasoning. Dehydrate 90 minutes, stirring occasionally. Allow to cool, then add cilantro and mint.

Lay coconut wrappers on a work surface. At one of the long ends, place 1 tablespoon of the filling and fold, diagonally, until a full triangular packet is completed. Reserve.

CHUTNEY Pulse-chop almonds in food processor; place in a bowl and set aside. Pulse-chop remaining ingredients in food processor; mix with almonds in bowl.

"YOGURT" Blend all ingredients in a Vita-Mix until smooth.

ASSEMBLY Interlock samosas on individual plates or a platter and spoon a generous amount of "yogurt" over them. Drizzle the chutney around the outside and garnish with mint leaves. YIELDS 16–20

white raisin shiitake dosas, cilantro cream, and ginger-tomato chutney

The first time I had a dosa, at Hampton Chutney in Soho, I wondered where they had been all these years. Dosas are so much fun to eat—and full of exotic tastes. I have always wondered why they aren't more popular. I use this variation whenever I have the opportunity. They are definitely far better when served directly from the dehydrator, still slightly warm, as they tend to be a bit chewy otherwise.

DOSAS
1^1/$_2$ cups flax meal
1 cup chopped yellow squash
^{1}/$_2$ cup chopped coconut meat
1 tablespoon fresh lemon juice
2 cups water
2 tablespoons raw agave
^{1}/$_2$ teaspoon salt
1 teaspoon cumin

FILLING
^{1}/$_2$ cup golden raisins
^{1}/$_2$ cup warm water
^{1}/$_4$ cup ginger juice
2 cups sliced shiitake mushrooms
1 teaspoon minced ginger
^{1}/$_4$ cup olive oil
Salt and pepper
^{1}/$_4$ cup chopped almonds

CHUTNEY
2 cups sun-dried tomatoes, reconstituted
^{1}/$_2$ shallot, chopped
2 Roma tomatoes, diced
2 tablespoons fresh lemon juice
^{1}/$_4$ cup olive oil
3 tablespoons raw agave
1 tablespoon salt
1 teaspoon chili pepper flakes
^{1}/$_4$ cup ginger juice

CREAM
1^1/$_2$ cups cashews, soaked 1–2 hours
^{1}/$_2$ cup coconut meat
^{1}/$_2$ cup water
^{1}/$_4$ cup lemon juice
^{1}/$_2$ teaspoon salt
^{1}/$_4$ cup cilantro

GARNISH
^{1}/$_4$ cup chopped almonds
Cilantro leaves

DOSAS Blend all ingredients in a Vita-Mix until smooth. Spread thinly into 6- to 7-inch rounds on dehydrator Teflex sheets. Dehydrate 5–6 hours until dry but very pliable.

FILLING Soak raisins in the water with ginger juice. Toss shiitake with minced ginger, olive oil, salt, and pepper, and dehydrate 1 hour. Drain raisins and combine with shiitake and almonds.

CHUTNEY Pulse-chop sun-dried tomatoes and shallot in a food processor. Place mixture in bowl with Roma tomatoes. Blend remaining ingredients in Vita-Mix until smooth; add to bowl. Stir until well combined.

CREAM Blend all ingredients except cilantro in Vita-Mix until smooth and creamy. Add cilantro and blend for a few moments until cilantro is well incorporated. Serve or store in refrigerator 3–4 days.

ASSEMBLY Fill dosas with raisin-shiitake mixture and gently fold closed. Place one dosa on each plate, top with chutney, and drizzle with cream. Garnish with nuts and cilantro. SERVES 4–6

creamy mango pudding, cardamom kulfi, and crispy lime macaroon

Kulfi is an Indian-style ice cream that is richer and creamier than regular ice cream, due to the lack of air that is whipped into traditional ice cream to make it lighter. The milk, traditionally from buffalo, is reduced by at least 50 percent before being incorporated into the recipe. Of course, in our raw version, we simply made a creamier nut-milk base with similar results.

PUDDING

2 cups coconut meat
2 cups chopped mango
1 cup water
$1/2$ cup raw agave
1 cup cashews, soaked 1–2 hours
1 tablespoon vanilla extract
1 tablespoon salt
2 tablespoons coconut oil
$1/2$ teaspoon cinnamon
$1/2$ teaspoon nutmeg

KULFI

$1/4$ cup coconut oil
1 cup coconut meat
$1/4$ cup raw agave
10 white cardamom pods
1 teaspoon rose water

MACAROON

$2^1/4$ cups coconut flakes
2 cups almond crumbs
1 cup almond flour
$1/4$ teaspoon sea salt
$1/4$ cup lime zest
$3/4$ cup maple syrup
$1/2$ cup coconut oil, melted
$1^1/2$ teaspoons vanilla extract

PUDDING Blend in a Vita-Mix and strain through a chinois. Chill, preferably overnight.

KULFI Blend all ingredients in Vita-Mix until smooth.

MACAROON Mix together dry ingredients. Add wet ingredients to dry mixture and mix thoroughly. Spread $1/2$ inch thick onto dehydrator Teflex sheets. Dehydrate 24–48 hours. Cut into desired shapes and transfer to dehydrator screens; —dehydrate another 8–10 hours.

ASSEMBLY Fill a 4-inch ring mold with pudding. Spread a thin layer of kulfi on the top, and garnish with a macaroon.
SERVES 4

apricot "yogurt" cake, sweet cream, pistachio tuiles, and anise syrup

When apricots are in season, buy them! I can have a bowl of several dozen in my home, and they'll never make it past three days. Fresh apricots are such a different temptation than dried, and their sweetness is so mild and intoxicating that you will keep taking another for quite some time before you realize what it is about them that is so addictive.

CAKE
3/4 cup cashews, soaked 1–2 hours
1 cup coconut meat
1 cup dried apricots, reconstituted
6 fresh apricots, pitted and roughly chopped
1/3 cup raw agave
1/4 cup coconut oil
Pinch salt
1/4 teaspoon vanilla extract
1/2 vanilla bean, scraped
Juice of 1/2 lime
1 teaspoon garam masala

CREAM
2 cups cashews, soaked 4 hours
1 cup coconut meat
1 tablespoon vanilla extract
1/2 teaspoon salt
1/2 cup raw agave

TUILES, OPTIONAL
1 1/4 cups flax meal
3/4 cup chopped pear
1/2 cup coconut meat
2 1/4 teaspoons fresh lemon juice
1 cup water
1 cup maple syrup
1/4 teaspoon salt
2 teaspoons vanilla
1 1/2 teaspoons garam masala
1 1/2 teaspoons cinnamon
3 cups pistachios, finely chopped to crumb form

SYRUP
1 cup raw agave
2 teaspoons cinnamon
1/2 teaspoon ground star anise
Pinch salt

CAKE Blend all ingredients in a Vita-Mix until smooth. Line a 10-inch cake pan with plastic wrap. Pour dough into pan. Refrigerate overnight.

CREAM Blend all ingredients in Vita-Mix until smooth.

TUILES Blend all ingredients in Vita-Mix until smooth. Spread thinly over dehydrator Teflex sheets. Dehydrate 5–6 hours until dry but very pliable. Remove from Teflex sheets and shape each round; if needed, use paper clips to secure the edges. Place cones on dehydrator screens and dehydrate another 24 hours until crisp. Remove paper clips.

SYRUP Blend all ingredients in Vita-Mix until smooth.

ASSEMBLY Cut the cake into squares; place a square on a dessert plate, pour anise syrup around edges of cake, and spoon several tablespoons of cream on top of each. Lean tuiles against side of cake. SERVES 4–6

Do not anticipate trouble
or worry about what
may never happen. Keep in the sunlight.
—Benjamin Franklin

radiance

The idea of spicy exotic food served in the open air, in close proximity to the sea, is an image that nearly anyone would feel positive about. Maybe it's the symbolic relationship of warm coastal climates to relaxing and eating well, but I have always been drawn to the flavors of sunny countries. The vibrancy of ingredients and sparkling clean flavors combined with a healthy dose of heat is a relentless charm.

A close friend once said to me that he always went to the sea to heal—and I have grown to realize that I am the same, if not in a medical sense, at least emotionally and physically to a large degree. The salty air, the sound of gentle waves, the rocky beaches, and the terrain of oceanfront land all provide a sense of health and, at the same time, exploration. My most positive moments—and my most productive, creative ones—are typically by the sea.

Naturally, the abundance of life, moving water, quick breezes, rapidly changing climates, and proliferation of wildlife and water fowl all combine to create an intoxicating energy that contributes to the cuisine of lands by the sea.

I was fortunate to grow up on a rocky New England coast. Little did I know how that would influence my life and career down the road. Today, I find its presence in nearly every aspect of what I do, physically or spiritually. Life has its way of creating circular paths, regardless of our chosen direction.

Much of my travel has been in the Mediterranean or on the coast of Latin and South America and other water-bordering regions of the United States. All foods have a life source, and I find that those prepared near the sea have more than their ample share. It is not only the ingredients but also the spirit that goes into their preparation as well as the sense of peace when consuming them.

The dishes in this section are recognized for their association with this spirit, for their ability to remind us of beautiful places visited in the past, and for the lifestyle they represent. They are most suitable to a summer afternoon luncheon, a dinner outdoors under the stars, a warm day, a casual celebration—and most of the food experiences we might associate with a slower, relaxing gathering.

caribbean conch chowder

The life of a food lover adds a great deal to one's memory; so often clouded by time and place, we develop taste memories that symbolize our experience with a dish. My first taste of conch was at a beach café in Mexico many years ago. I spent a long day in the sun reading *Tender is the Night,* so immersed in the book that I felt as if I were on the beach next to the divers. After a couple of iced margaritas, the chilled conch was impeccable. I never had it again, but this version succeeded in recapturing that moment for me. Not only did I love the flavor of this chowder, I also loved being transported back to a quieter, relaxing time in my life.

CREAM
1 cup Brazil nuts, soaked 8–12 hours
3 cups water
2 tablespoons olive oil
2 tablespoons fresh lemon juice
1 tablespoon nama shoyu
1 shallot
1 teaspoon nutritional yeast

2 teaspoons salt
Black pepper
$1/2$ teaspoon chili powder
Pinch cayenne

ASSEMBLY
2 cups chopped young Thai coconut meat
$1/2$ cup diced red bell pepper
$1/2$ cup minced celery
2 tablespoons minced scallions

CREAM Blend Brazil nuts and water in a Vita-Mix. Strain through a fine strainer and discard the pulp. Blend this nut milk and the remaining ingredients in Vita-Mix until completely smooth and creamy. Taste for seasoning.

ASSEMBLY Divide the soup among 4 bowls and garnish right before serving with the ingredients listed.

NOTE: When I first served this dish at a Caribbean dinner, we poured the soup inside young coconuts with the flesh still intact. The presentation is always fun, and the fresh tender coconut meat is great when scooped out and eaten with the chowder. SERVES 4–6

roasted sweet pepper soup, basil manti, and hazelnut "yogurt"

Red sweet peppers (longer and thinner skinned than red bell peppers) are ideal for making soups in the summer, when they are sweet and combine well with spices, nuts, and herbs. I was fortunate to have a consulting position in Istanbul many years ago, when I became close friends with the family I was working with, who owned the Borsa Restaurant group. They are the most hospitable people I have ever met and always went out of their way not only to feed me well but also to educate me on their native cuisine. Turkey is one of few countries that produces all of its own food, and the ingredients are impeccable. Manti are dumplings, traditionally filled with lamb and served in a yogurt sauce. As always, we've reinterpreted everything and came up with a dish that was everyone's favorite.

SOUP (2 QUARTS)
1 cup cashews, soaked 1–2 hours
5 cups water
1 cup coconut meat
$3^1/_2$ teaspoons salt
Black pepper
2 teaspoons fresh lemon juice
1 teaspoon nutritional yeast
2 pinches cayenne pepper
$3/_4$ teaspoon Aleppo pepper spice
2 cups red bell pepper pieces, dehydrated 2 hours

WRAPPERS
2 cups coconut meat
$1/_2$ cup fresh basil leaves
1 tablespoon water
Pinch salt

FILLING
2 cups roughly chopped portobello mushrooms
$1/_2$ cup roughly chopped red onions
Olive oil
Salt
Black pepper
$1/_2$ cup cashews, soaked 1–2 hours
1 teaspoon chopped thyme

"YOGURT"
$1^3/_4$ cups hazelnuts, soaked 1–2 hours
$1/_2$ cup coconut meat
$3/_4$ cup water
$1/_3$ cup fresh lemon juice
$1/_4$ teaspoon salt

GARNISH
Chervil

SOUP Blend all ingredients in a Vita-Mix until smooth. Warm in a dehydrator until ready to serve.

WRAPPERS Blend all ingredients in Vita-Mix until very smooth. Using an offset spatula, spread the mixture thinly on dehydrator Teflex sheets and dehydrate at 115 degrees F for 3–4 hours, or until the surface is dry. Carefully flip over and remove from Teflex. Wrappers should be pliable and completely dry. On a flat surface, trim the edges and cut into 9 equal squares.

FILLING Toss portobello mushrooms and onions with olive oil (just to coat), salt, and pepper. Dehydrate 30–40 minutes. Pulse in a food processor with cashews and thyme to chop into small pieces and set aside.

"YOGURT" Blend all ingredients in Vita-Mix until smooth and creamy. Store in refrigerator and bring back to room temperature before serving.

ASSEMBLY Place $1^1/_2$ teaspoons of manti filling in center of wrapper. Moisten edges. Gently fold four corners to meet in center. Lightly press. Divide soup among 4 bowls and gently place 2 dumplings in each. Garnish with chervil and spoon a generous amount of "yogurt" into soup. SERVES 4–6

NOTE: These wrappers can be prepared in advance and stored in the refrigerator for quite some time. I have found that they remain fresh for a couple of weeks (perhaps longer, but they never last that long without someone eating them first) and are easily used as a wrapper for anything when you would like to prepare a quick lunch or snack. They should be well sealed in plastic wrap and kept dry. Remove them from the refrigerator at least 20 minutes before handling so that they become more pliable.

spinach and beet ravioli, cashew "ricotta," wilted spinach with basil, and wine pear sauce

In my early years with raw food, this same combination of ingredients may have resulted in a raw beet filled with a seasoned cashew purée, but this version is a well-tuned example of how far raw food has progressed. A standard coconut wrapper infused with spinach and beet creates a brilliant color contrast but is also a light, delicious base for the creamy cashew purée, chewy and tangy spinach, and the sweet pear sauce. I found it to be one of the most well-balanced dishes to come from my kitchen, and it is now something I serve whenever I have the opportunity.

RAVIOLI
2 cups chopped coconut meat, divided
2 tablespoons spinach juice
$1/4$ teaspoon salt, divided
2 tablespoons beet juice

"RICOTTA"
$3^1/2$ cups cashews, soaked 1–2 hours
$1/4$ cup fresh lemon juice
$1/2$ cup water
1 cup olive oil
$1^1/2$ teaspoons salt
2 teaspoons nutritional yeast

SAUCE
$2^1/2$ pears, peeled, cored, and chopped
$1/4$ teaspoon salt
$1/4$ cup raw agave
$1/2$ cup white wine

SPINACH
2 quarts torn spinach
1 quart fresh basil leaves
Olive oil
Salt

GARNISH
Fresh basil

RAVIOLI Blend half the coconut with spinach juice and half the salt in a Vita-Mix until very smooth. Spread very thin on dehydrator Teflex sheets and dehydrate 3–4 hours. Repeat the process with the beet version, using the beet juice instead of spinach. Remove from Teflex and trim edges. Cut into 9 squares.

"RICOTTA" Process all ingredients in a food processor 3–5 minutes until smooth.

SAUCE Blend all ingredients in Vita-Mix until smooth. Prior to serving, place in a dehydrator for 20–30 minutes at 115 degrees F to warm.

SPINACH Toss all ingredients in a medium-size bowl. Let sit for 30 minutes in a warm place.

ASSEMBLY Assemble the ravioli by placing 1 teaspoon "ricotta" on half the spinach and half the beet raviolis. Wet corners slightly and press remaining pasta squares on top of the same color wrappers—press tightly.

Spoon sauce onto plates, keeping it away from edges, and place 2 spinach and 2 beet ravioli on each plate. Garnish with wilted spinach and fresh basil. SERVES 4–6

arugula gnocchi, sweet pepper sauce, marinated asparagus, and pine nut "parmesan"

Shortly after beginning my first real restaurant job at the Sicilian restaurant Malvasia, I happened to be in the right place at the right time. The chef, Gennaro Picone, was a master with pasta, and every dish on his menu was outstanding. Most were light, but his gnocchi were rich and delicious. They were a bright green from subtly steamed spinach and were like eating green clouds—they were even good plain and cold, not to mention how they were with the woodsy porcini mushrooms and Gorgonzola cream that he served them with. In the time I worked there, I often tried preparing gnocchi at home, but they were never the same. It takes a very light touch and a lot of practice to make a proper gnocchi, and the creation of this dish certainly held up to the challenge I expected.

GNOCCHI
2 cups chopped jicama, processed in food processor
  and strained
1 cup cashews, soaked 1–2 hours
$3/4$ teaspoon sea salt
$1/2$ teaspoon nutritional yeast
$1/3$ cup fresh lemon juice
Black pepper
$1/4$ cup cashew flour
$1/2$ cup chopped arugula

SAUCE
1 cup cashews, soaked 1–2 hours
1 cup diced red bell pepper, dehydrated 12 hours
$1/4$ cup coconut meat

$1/4$ fresh red bell pepper, chopped
$1/2$ cup olive oil
2 teaspoons salt
Black pepper
2 teaspoons fresh lemon juice
1 pinch cayenne pepper

ASPARAGUS
$1/2$ bunch asparagus
Olive oil
Salt
Black pepper

"PARMESAN"
(see page 22)

GNOCCHI Mix first 6 ingredients in a large bowl. Blend in batches in a Vita-Mix until very smooth. Place mixture in large bowl and stir in cashew flour and arugula by hand. Shape into gnocchi and gently roll on dehydrator screens to create gnocchi pattern. Place in dehydrator for 2–3 hours or until crust forms around outside. Serve immediately or warm in dehydrator until ready to serve.

SAUCE Blend all ingredients in Vita-Mix until smooth. Warm in dehydrator until ready to serve.

ASPARAGUS Cut the asparagus on a bias into $1\frac{1}{2}$-inch lengths. Toss with olive oil, salt, and pepper. Dehydrate on Teflex sheets for 30–40 minutes.

ASSEMBLY Coat the bottom of the plate with sauce. Place gnocchi on sauce, and garnish with asparagus and "Parmesan." SERVES 4–6

creamy eggplant and hummus cream in almond tart shells with green olive tapenade

The first taste of this dish took me on a culinary journey backward around the world. My first sous chef was Malcolm Johnson, one of a few mad scientists that I would have the good fortune of working with over the years. He introduced me to this green olive tapenade at my first restaurant and it has followed me over the years, first with tuna tartare, then with a charcoal grilled vegetable pizza, and now this raw dish. The almond crust is purely Moroccan, the Hummus very much from the Eastern Mediterranean—and the dish as a whole, quite New York.

TART SHELLS
1 cup almonds, processed to crumb form
$1/4$ cup cashew flour
1 teaspoon salt
$1^1/2$ teaspoons nutritional yeast
1 tablespoon olive oil
2 tablespoons water
$1^1/2$ teaspoons cumin

CREAM
$1/2$ cup cashews, soaked 1–2 hours
$1/4$ cup macadamia nuts, soaked 1–2 hours
1 tablespoon fresh lemon juice
2 teaspoons olive oil

4 tablespoons tahini
$1/2$ teaspoon salt
4 tablespoons water
1 clove garlic

TAPENADE
$1/2$ cup pitted green olives
2 tablespoons fresh lemon juice
3 tablespoons olive oil
Pinch anise seed

EGGPLANT
1 large eggplant, chopped
2 tablespoons olive oil
Pinch salt
Pinch pepper
1 teaspoon garam masala

TART SHELLS Mix all ingredients in a bowl with hands. Use your fingers to press into plastic-lined individual tart shells ($3^1/2$- to 4-inch diameter with removable bottoms) and dehydrate overnight. Carefully remove the crusts from the shells, place them back on the dehydrator screen, and continue dehydrating until slightly crisp.

CREAM Blend all ingredients in a Vita-Mix until completely smooth. Store in the refrigerator and bring back to room temperature before serving.

TAPENADE Blend in Vita-Mix until smooth.

EGGPLANT Toss eggplant with olive oil, salt, pepper, and garam masala. Dehydrate until soft.

ASSEMBLY Place the tart shell on the plate and fill with the cream. Top with the eggplant and drizzle with the tapenade.
SERVES 4–6

golden and green cannelloni with sun-dried tomato–ginger marinara, mint-basil pistachio pesto, green zebra tomatoes, and pine nut and black truffle "ricotta"

The first raw food dish (or at least, the first successful raw food dish) that I ever created was a green zebra tomato lasagna that I designed for my first raw food menu. There was never a single evening that it wasn't the best-selling dish on the menu, which lies in the fact that it offers familiar flavors in a unique form. Raw food can often be intimidating, especially for those who have never tried it, and the components of this dish resemble a welcoming gesture—tomato sauce, pesto, ricotta, tomatoes. They work together, we've all tried them, and the dish is full flavored.

CANNELLONI
1 golden zucchini
2 green zucchini
Olive oil
Salt
2 green zebra tomatoes, sliced

"RICOTTA"
2 cups pine nuts, soaked 1–2 hours
2 tablespoons nutritional yeast
$1/4$ cup fresh lemon juice
2 tablespoons black truffle oil
$1/4$ cup water
$1/2$ teaspoon salt
2 tablespoons chopped fresh thyme
2 tablespoons chopped scallions

PESTO
$1/2$ cup packed fresh basil leaves
$1/2$ cup packed fresh mint leaves

$1/4$ cup pistachios
$1/3$ cup olive oil
$1/2$ teaspoon salt
Pinch black pepper

MARINARA
$1^1/2$ cups sun-dried tomatoes, soaked 1 hour
$1/2$ Roma tomato, roughly chopped
$1/4$ shallot, chopped
1 tablespoon lemon juice
$1/4$ cup olive oil
2 teaspoons agave
$1^1/2$ teaspoons salt
$1/4$ cup ginger juice
Pinch dried chili pepper flakes

ASSEMBLY
Olive oil
Fresh basil leaves or lavender sprigs

CANNELLONI Using a mandoline, cut the zucchini lengthwise into very thin slices. Brush slices with olive oil and sprinkle with a little salt.

"RICOTTA" Pulse nuts in a food processor to break up. Add yeast, lemon juice, oil, and water; blend until smooth. Add salt, thyme, and scallions; pulse until well combined. Store in the refrigerator and bring back to room temperature before serving.

PESTO Place all ingredients in food processor and process until chunky. Store in the refrigerator; bring back to room temperature before serving.

MARINARA Squeeze water from sun-dried tomatoes and place all ingredients in food processor. Process until smooth. Store in refrigerator; bring back to room temperature before serving.

ASSEMBLY Overlap 2 green zucchini slices flat on a work surface, with the ends facing you. Place 2 tablespoons "ricotta" close to the near end; top with 2 tablespoons marinara sauce, 1 tablespoon pesto, and green zebra tomatoes. Roll carefully 3 times, forming a rectangle, and place on the plate. Form gently with hands to shape it. Repeat the same steps with the golden zucchini. Place two green cannelloni and one yellow on each plate. Drizzle with olive oil and garnish with basil or lavender. SERVES 4–6

pine nut tartlet, basil "crème fraîche," and sweet tomatoes

I was ready to give up on this dish at one point due to its delicacy—but I pursued it relentlessly and will be forever grateful. It's actually an easy dish to make but should only be attempted when you can find small, fresh, sweet tomatoes at their peak. This remains a recipe that was so clean and vivid that I can easily taste it as I think back to the day I first had it. The variations that are possible for this dish are endless, from doing a different herb or green cream, to the large possibilities of fresh vegetables it could be topped with, ranging from summer squash, fava beans, sweet marinated peas, and radishes.

TART SHELLS
1 cup pine nuts, processed to crumb form
$1/4$ cup almond flour
$1/4$ teaspoon salt
$1/2$ teaspoon nutritional yeast
1 tablespoon olive oil
2 tablespoons water

"CRÈME FRAÎCHE"
$1^1/2$ cups cashews, soaked 1–2 hours
$1/2$ cup water

$3/4$ cup fresh lemon juice
2 teaspoons nutritional yeast
$1/4$ cup fresh basil

TOMATOES
1 pint baby heirloom tomatoes, halved
3 tablespoons olive oil
Pinch salt

GARNISH
Micro basil sprigs

TART SHELLS Place all ingredients in a bowl and combine using your hands. Use your fingers to press into plastic-lined individual tart shells ($3^1/2$- to 4-inch diameter, with removable bottoms) and dehydrate overnight. Carefully remove the crusts from the shells, place them back in the dehydrator, and continue dehydrating until slightly crisp.

"CRÈME FRAÎCHE" Blend all ingredients in a Vita-Mix until smooth and creamy. Store in the refrigerator until firm.

TOMATOES Toss tomatoes with olive oil and salt.

ASSEMBLY Place the tart shell on a plate and fill with the "crème fraîche." Top with baby tomatoes and garnish with micro basil sprigs. SERVES 4–6

shiitake moqueca and coconut "rice"

Moqueca has a long history with our kitchen—my first job as a chef was with a Brazilian restaurant company, and the owners, in their efforts to educate me about their native cuisine, sent me to Rio de Janeiro to learn how to prepare many of their classics, including this great dish. One of my recent sous chefs is also from Rio, and this recipe is her version—far more authentic than mine and quite delicious.

"RICE"
4 cups peeled and roughly chopped jicama
$1/2$ cup coconut meat
2 tablespoons coconut water
$1^1/2$ teaspoons raw agave
$1^1/2$ teaspoons fresh lime juice
$1/4$ teaspoon salt
1 teaspoon coriander
1 pinch cayenne

MOQUECA SAUCE
$1/2$ red onion, chopped
$1^1/2$ tomatoes, seeded and diced
$1/4$ bunch cilantro
1 tablespoon green onion
1 tablespoon parsley
$1/3$ cup carrot juice

$2/3$ cup coconut milk ($1/2$ cup coconut meat and $1/4$ cup water)
$1/2$ teaspoon salt
1 teaspoon cayenne pepper
Black pepper

MUSHROOMS
2 cups thinly sliced shiitake mushrooms
Olive oil
Salt and pepper

TOMATOES
2 cups cherry tomatoes
Olive oil
Salt and pepper
$1/4$ cup finely chopped cilantro

GARNISH
Cilantro

"RICE" Process jicama in a food processor until a rice-like consistency is achieved. Press out excess liquid with a cheesecloth or through a sieve. Place in a medium-size bowl and set aside. Blend remaining ingredients in a Vita-Mix until smooth and creamy. Add to jicama and combine well. Store in the refrigerator until ready to serve. Bring back to room temperature before serving.

MOQUECA SAUCE Blend all ingredients in Vita-Mix. Set aside.

MUSHROOMS Toss mushrooms with olive oil, salt and pepper. Place on Teflex sheets and dehydrate 30–45 minutes.

TOMATOES Toss tomatoes with olive oil, salt, and pepper. Place on Teflex sheets and dehydrate 30–45 minutes.

ASSEMBLY Place $1/4$ cup coconut rice off center of plate and top with cilantro. Pour sauce on plate, top with shiitake mushrooms, and garnish with tomatoes and cilantro.
SERVES 4–6

> "The greatest revolution of our generation is the discovery that human beings, by changing the inner attitudes of their minds, can change the outer aspects of their lives."
>
> —William James

revolution

Revolution is something that we, as chefs working with raw organic food, deal with on a daily basis. We are in the midst of one, whether we speak of it or not. A revolution is a turn, a rotation, a change of events that is hopefully (and often) leading to improved conditions. Fortunately, we are blessed with countless sources of superior organic products to prepare our meals with. On the other hand, the food supply chain is riddled with genetically modified ingredients that are shipped from afar, treated with massive amounts of pesticides, and bear little more than a passing resemblance to the fruit or vegetable that they are attempting to imitate. There is a large and growing diversity with how we eat. I see this as a positive sign in many ways, given that the factions at least exist—there is resistance, and ultimately (or at least hopefully) wise choices will prevail.

We embrace revolution for the positive change it may often bring—that is not always the case, but it certainly offers passion, energy, and choice. Many of my dishes are inspired by countries that have been through everything from prosperity, hardship, and struggle in the face of revolution—there is always a sense of pride and thankfulness following such a struggle. It may be our own ability to romanticize history, but we often find that any kitchen becomes most inspired by the foods of these nations—meaningful cuisine with a long history and sensibility—foods that, when prepared in a modern kitchen, become very modern and yet still retain the charm of old-world cuisine.

Revolutions accelerate change, and as change relates to food today, that acceleration is necessary. A staid approach, ignoring the obvious signals from every direction, may lead to peril of one degree or another, whereas the old adage "change is good" has never been more appropriate. We love the idea of fighting for truth, living for health, reaching for meaning, and, most of all, preparing great meals. Let us all forge that path.

The recipes in this chapter embrace revolutionary intellect in the culinary world.

empanada de espinaca y salsa de tomate: empanada with spinach, tomato relish, and cilantro-mint purée

Cuban empanadas are usually filled with seasoned meats. Of course, that won't happen with raw foods, but the concept remains intact. I like serving empanadas as a filled pastry—a casual bite or light meal with a salad. The cilantro-mint purée is an important element in this recipe, as they otherwise may be a bit dry.

PASTRY
3/4 cup flax meal
3 cups corn kernels
1 cup water
2 tablespoons olive oil
2 teaspoons cumin
1/2 small red onion, roughly chopped
1 clove garlic
3/4 teaspoon salt
1 tablespoon fresh lime juice
Pinch cayenne

FILLING
3 cups pine nuts, soaked 1–2 hours
3 tablespoons fresh lemon juice
1 teaspoon salt
3/4 teaspoon nutritional yeast
2 whole scallions

SPINACH
1 quart torn spinach
Olive oil to coat
Salt

RELISH
2 cups finely diced tomatoes
1/4 cup finely diced onions
1 tablespoon olive oil
1/4 cup chopped parsley
2 teaspoons dried oregano
1 tablespoon fresh lime juice
1 teaspoon lime zest

PURÉE
1 cup fresh cilantro
1 cup fresh mint
1 cup olive oil
Salt

GARNISH
Cilantro sprigs

PASTRY Set flax meal aside. Place remaining ingredients in a food processor and blend until smooth. Stir in flax meal. Spread batter onto Teflex sheets in 3-inch circles and dehydrate at 118 degrees F for about 3–4 hours, or until able to flip. Flip rounds onto dehydrator screens and place another screen on top to hold rounds in place; dehydrate an additional 45–60 minutes, or until they are dry but still pliable.

FILLING Process all ingredients except scallions in food processor until smooth. Add scallions and pulse until they have broken up and are well combined. Store in a container in the refrigerator.

SPINACH Toss all ingredients in a medium-size bowl. Let sit 30 minutes or cover with plastic wrap and dehydrate 20 minutes.

RELISH Mix all ingredients in a large bowl.

PURÉE Blend all ingredients in a Vita-Mix until smooth.

ASSEMBLY Spread filling on the side of pastry that is completely dry; top with spinach. Fold pastry in half over filling and secure edges tightly by pressing with the tines of a fork. You may need to wet edges with water before pressing with fork to secure well. Place back on dehydrator screens and dehydrate 15–20 minutes until the outside is completely dry. Place empanadas on the plate and drizzle with purée. Serve with the tomato relish on the side and garnish with cilantro sprigs. SERVES 4–6

hallacas vegetarianas: vegetable tamales with tomato-chile sauce

These tiny tamales, wrapped in a strand of corn dyed with beet juice, are so charming that they would be delicious filled with air—yet, the filling has a very silky body and deep flavor that is surprising, given the lack of heavy fats or dairy.

FILLING
1 quart corn, divided
$1^1/_4$ cups minced tomatoes
$1^1/_2$ cups minced red bell pepper
6 tablespoons sun-dried tomatoes, soaked
$1^1/_4$ cups pine nuts, soaked 1–2 hours
$1^1/_4$ cups cashews, soaked 1–2 hours
1 teaspoon sea salt
$3/_4$ teaspoon nutritional yeast
2 tablespoons minced red onion
2 tablespoons stemmed and chopped fresh cilantro
1 clove garlic, peeled and minced
$3/_4$ cup fresh lime juice

SAUCE
2 cups sun-dried tomatoes, soaked 1 hour
1 ancho chile, soaked 10–15 minutes
1 Roma tomato, diced

$1/_2$ shallot, chopped
2 tablespoons fresh lemon juice
$1/_4$ cup olive oil
4 teaspoons raw agave
2 teaspoons salt
Pinch chile pepper flakes

"SOUR CREAM"
1 cup cashews, soaked 1–2 hours
$1/_2$ cup water
$1/_4$ cup olive oil
$4^1/_2$ teaspoons fresh lemon juice
$3/_4$ teaspoon salt

ASSEMBLY
12–18 corn husks
1 cup beet juice
Corn husk "strings" (strands torn from ends of husks)
Ancho chile powder

FILLING Place 2 cups corn, the tomatoes, and the red bell pepper in a bowl; set aside. In a food processor, blend the remaining corn and ingredients until very smooth. Pour into the bowl with corn, tomatoes, and red bell pepper, and mix well with hands. Store in refrigerator.

SAUCE Squeeze water from sun-dried tomatoes and ancho chile. Place all ingredients in a Vita-Mix and blend until smooth. Store in refrigerator.

"SOUR CREAM" Blend all ingredients in Vita-Mix until completely smooth. Store in refrigerator.

ASSEMBLY Tear 24–36 strings from corn husks and place in a bowl with beet juice. Place strings on dehydrator screens for 20 minutes to dry. Soak corn husks in water 30 minutes and dry well. Place 2–3 tablespoons tamale filling in the middle of each husk and tie both edges with strings. Place 3 tamales on each plate. Serve with sauce and "sour cream." Sprinkle with ancho chile powder. SERVES 4–6

picadillo santiaguero, arroz amarillo, y mariquitas: portobello-meat stew with yellow "rice," crisp plantain, and macadamia "sour cream"

Picadillo is a stew-like dish served in Latin America, traditionally with beef. This version uses the meaty portobello mushroom instead. The Cuban version of this dish has olives, as does this recipe. It can be eaten on its own with "rice" but the mixture can also be eaten in a taco shell.

PICADILLO
4 cups chopped portobello mushrooms
$1/4$ cup green or black olives, pitted and chopped
Olive oil
Salt
Black pepper
2 tablespoons sun-dried tomatoes, soaked, drained, and chopped
$1/4$ cup raisins, soaked
$1/4$ cup chopped green bell pepper
Pinch sea salt

YELLOW "RICE"
4 cups chopped jicama
1 cup coconut meat
6 tablespoons carrot juice
1 tablespoon raw agave
1 tablespoon fresh lime juice

$1/2$ teaspoon turmeric
Pinch salt
Pinch cayenne

PLANTAIN
1 plantain
Coconut oil to brush
Salt

"SOUR CREAM"
1 cup macadamia nuts, soaked 1–2 hours
$1/2$ cup water
$1/4$ cup olive oil
$4^1/2$ teaspoons fresh lemon juice
$3/4$ teaspoon salt

GARNISH
$1/2$ cup "sour cream" (see above)
Cilantro sprigs

PICADILLO Toss portobello mushrooms and green peppers in olive oil. Place on Teflex sheets and dehydrate 45–60 minutes. Combine remaining ingredients and mix well. Dehydrate together another 30 minutes and reserve.

YELLOW "RICE" Pulse-chop jicama in a food processor until ricelike consistency is achieved. Blend remaining ingredients in a Vita-Mix until very smooth. Mix with yellow "rice." Set aside.

PLANTAIN Slice plantain on a diagonal into thin slices. Brush with coconut oil and sprinkle with salt. Place on dehydrator screens and dehydrate until crisp.

"SOUR CREAM" Blend all ingredients in Vita-Mix until completely smooth. Store in refrigerator.

ASSEMBLY Place a ring mold in the center of a plate. Fill with ¼ cup yellow "rice" and press. Put ¼ cup picadillo on top and gently press. Carefully remove the ring mold. Stick in 5 plantain chips. Using a squeeze bottle, drizzle with "sour cream" and garnish with cilantro sprigs. Repeat for remaining 3 servings. SERVES 4

natilla de chocolate, majarete y turron de coco: chocolate pudding, sweet corn flan, coffee-cinnamon syrup, and crispy chile macaroons

If every dessert were simply chocolate or fruit, life in the kitchen might not be that entertaining. Whenever possible, we like to incorporate vegetables or herbs into a dessert in a subtle way as a means to offer our guests a challenging flavor, something new, and a dessert that they will remember us by—hopefully in a fond way.

PUDDING
$3/4$ cup cashews, soaked 1–2 hours
$3/4$ cup coconut meat
6 tablespoons water
$1/2$ cup raw agave
6 tablespoons melted coconut oil
$1/2$ teaspoon vanilla extract
$1/4$ teaspoon sea salt
$1/2$ cup cocoa powder
$3/4$ teaspoon raw carob powder

FLAN
$3/4$ cup fresh yellow corn
$3/4$ cup cashews, soaked
$1/2$ cup coconut meat
$1/2$ teaspoon vanilla extract
$1/4$ teaspoon salt
$1/4$ cup raw agave
6 tablespoons coconut oil
6 tablespoons coconut flour
$1/2$ teaspoon cinnamon

MACAROONS
1 cup coconut flakes, ground to powder
1 cup cashew flour
$1/2$ cup flax meal
$3/4$ teaspoon cinnamon
1 teaspoon ancho chile powder
Pinch salt
6 tablespoons maple syrup
2 tablespoons coconut oil, melted
$3/4$ teaspoon vanilla extract

SYRUP
$1/2$ cup raw agave
1 teaspoon cinnamon
$1/2$ teaspoon coffee extract
$1/4$ vanilla bean, scraped
Pinch salt

GARNISH
$1/4$ cup fresh corn
Mint sprigs

PUDDING Blend all ingredients in a Vita-Mix until completely smooth. Place in refrigerator for 5–6 hours or freeze for 1–2 hours prior to serving.

FLAN Blend all ingredients until smooth in Vita-Mix. Pour into small ramekins; refrigerate 5–6 hours or freeze 1–2 hours prior to serving.

MACAROONS Mix together dry ingredients. Add wet ingredients to dry mixture and mix thoroughly. Spread $1/2$ inch thick onto dehydrator Teflex sheets. Dehydrate 24–48 hours. Cut into desired shapes and transfer to dehydrator screens; dehydrate another 8–10 hours.

SYRUP Blend ingredients until smooth in Vita-Mix.

ASSEMBLY Place 1 scoop flan and a quenelle of pudding on each plate. Arrange with macaroons and corn; garnish with mint and drizzle with syrup. SERVES 4–6

chile rellenos, monta-raw jack "cheese," and cacao mole

This dish was first prepared by Kristen Reyes and Justin Baumgartner for a Mexican dinner I was hosting. When I first saw it, I could not believe the colors—bright green pepper offset by an orange cheese, golden corn filling, and chocolate mole—and it tastes every bit as complex and satisfying as it appears. I would venture to say that, strictly as a consumer, this would be my favorite dish to enjoy with a good glass of wine.

RELLENOS FILLING
2 cups fresh corn
2 cups sliced and quartered zucchini
1 cup diced red bell pepper
1 cup diced tomato
$3/4$ cup minced red onion
1 tablespoon minced jalapeño
1 tablespoon chopped fresh cilantro
1 tablespoon fresh lime juice
$1/4$ teaspoon cumin
Pinch cayenne
Pinch chili powder
Salt and black pepper to taste

"CHEESE"
$3^{1}/2$ cups macadamia nuts, soaked 1–2 hours
$3/4$ cup olive oil
$1/4$ shallot, diced
1 clove garlic
2 tablespoons fresh lemon juice
1 tablespoon sea salt
3 tablespoons nutritional yeast
$3/4$ teaspoon chili powder
Pinch cayenne

CACAO MOLE
2 dried ancho or chipotle chiles, soaked 2–3 hours
$1/4$ cup chopped red onion

1 clove garlic
1 tablespoon sunflower seeds, soaked 4–6 hours
$1/4$ cup almond butter
$1/4$ cup raisins, soaked 20–30 minutes
3 tablespoons olive oil
$1/2$ cup water
2 tablespoons raw agave
$1/2$ cup cacao powder
1 teaspoon ground cumin
$1/4$ teaspoon ground coriander
$1/2$ teaspoon salt
Pinch cayenne
Black pepper to taste

RED PEPPER SAUCE
2 cups chopped red bell peppers
1 red chile pepper, seeded and minced
$1/2$ cup cashews, soaked 2 hours
$1/4$ cup water
1 tablespoon fresh lime juice
2 tablespoons raw agave
Salt to taste

GARNISH
4–6 fresh poblano or Anaheim chiles or red lipstick peppers

RELLENOS FILLING Combine all ingredients in a bowl and let sit 15–20 minutes prior to using.

"CHEESE" Place all ingredients in a food processor. Allow to process up to 5 minutes; scrape sides of processor with a spatula to be sure all ingredients are completely combined.

CACAO MOLE Blend all ingredients in a Vita-Mix until smooth.

RED PEPPER SAUCE Blend all ingredients in Vita-Mix until smooth.

ASSEMBLY Cut the chiles or peppers in half and stuff each with equal amounts of "cheese" and rellenos filling. Place stuffed chiles on a sheet pan, cover with plastic wrap, and dehydrate 2–3 hours. Serve warm with cacao mole and red pepper sauce. SERVES 4–6

chocolate ancho chile tarts with lime-spiced mango chutney and cinnamon vanilla cream

I love chocolate and spice or chocolate and salt—perhaps that is why mole is one of my favorite things to eat and the reason I always keep a Jacques Torres "Wicked Chocolate" bar in my kitchen. In this dish, the unexpected spice kick is nicely offset by the cooling quality of the crème anglaise.

TART CRUST
Coconut oil
2 cups Cookie Crumb Flour (see below)

COOKIE CRUMB FLOUR
4 cups cocoa powder
4 cups oat flour
1 cup maple syrup
1 cup agave
3 tablespoons coconut oil, melted
1^1/$_2$ teaspoons Himalayan salt
1^1/$_2$ teaspoons vanilla extract

TART FILLING
1^1/$_2$ cups cashews, soaked
^{1}/$_2$ cup plus 2 tablespoons water
^{1}/$_2$ cup plus 2 tablespoons raw agave
^{1}/$_2$ cup melted coconut oil
^{1}/$_2$ teaspoon vanilla extract
^{1}/$_4$ teaspoon sea salt
^{1}/$_2$ cup plus 2 tablespoons cocoa powder
2 tablespoons ancho chile powder

CHUTNEY, OPTIONAL
1 quart frozen mango, chopped
^{1}/$_2$ cup raw agave
^{1}/$_2$ cup fresh lime juice
^{1}/$_4$ teaspoon ancho chile powder plus more to taste
Pinch cayenne plus more to taste
2 tablespoons lime zest plus more to taste

VANILLA CREAM
^{1}/$_2$ cup cashews, soaked 1–2 hours
^{1}/$_4$ cup coconut meat
^{1}/$_4$ cup raw agave
^{3}/$_4$ cup water
1 teaspoon vanilla extract
^{1}/$_4$ cup coconut oil
^{1}/$_2$ teaspoon cinnamon
Pinch cayenne
Pinch sea salt

TART CRUST Mix enough coconut oil into the cookie flour until it holds together. Press very thin into tart shells and chill in freezer before filling.

COOKIE CRUMB FLOUR Mix dry ingredients thoroughly. Add remaining ingredients to dry ingredients. Mix well with hands. Crumble into small pieces (no bigger than ^{1}/$_2$ inch) onto dehydrator screens. Dehydrate 3 days. Process in a food processor until it reaches a small crumb consistency. Sift to separate crumbs from flour. Crumbs should be no larger than ^{1}/$_4$ inch. Store crumbs and flour in separate containers in refrigerator.

TART FILLING Blend all ingredients in a Vita-Mix until very smooth. Fill cookie crusts and chill in freezer overnight. Re-

move tarts from metal shells and wrap in plastic wrap. Store in freezer.

CHUTNEY Place all ingredients in a quart container, then put in a dehydrator at 115 degrees F for 3–4 hours. When mango is thawed and warm, strain and toss with a bit more ancho chile powder, cayenne, and lime zest. Pulse-chop in a food processor to create a very chunky compote.

VANILLA CREAM Blend all ingredients in Vita-Mix until very smooth. Refrigerate until ready to serve.

ASSEMBLY Pour a generous pool of cream on plates, place a tart on top and spoon optional chutney on tarts. SERVES 4

oyster mushroom seviche
and bitter orange–lime sauce

The chewy oyster mushrooms are treated in the same way that a traditional recipe would call for marinating fish or shellfish—"cooking" with the acidic component in citrus while absorbing the flavors it sits with. I love marinated oyster mushrooms and find their flavor more pleasant than raw shiitake, which sometimes have a musty taste I don't care for.

SEVICHE
$1/4$ cup finely chopped red onion
$1/2$ cup peeled, seeded, and diced fresh plum tomatoes
$1/2$ medium habanero chile, seeds and ribs removed, chopped into tiny pieces
$3/4$ cup fresh-squeezed orange juice, strained

$1/4$ cup fresh-squeezed lime juice, strained
Pinch salt
2 cups oyster mushrooms, torn into thirds lengthwise
1 large avocado, peeled and cut into medium-size dice
4 orange wedges for garnish
4 lime wedges for garnish
Chopped cilantro leaves

SEVICHE In a bowl, mix the onion, tomatoes, habanero, orange juice, lime juice, and salt. Add the oyster mushrooms and mix. Cover very tightly with plastic wrap and refrigerate 2 hours. Add the avocado and mix carefully so it doesn't fall apart. Serve in medium-size martini glasses garnished with an orange wedge, lime wedge, and chopped cilantro.
SERVES 4

tricolor sesame-cashew dumplings and sweet chile–lime sauce

These beautiful dumplings appear like flowers on a large tray. They were originally an idea put together for a large party I catered in the summer for seven hundred people. The only problem with these dumplings is that they will disappear before a server can get more than five feet past the kitchen—guests devour them by the handful!

WRAPPERS
3 cups chopped coconut meat, divided
$1/2$ teaspoon sea salt, divided
$1/4$ cup each beet, carrot, and spinach juice

FILLING
4 cups cashews, soaked 1–2 hours
$1/4$ cup nama shoyu
$1/4$ cup sesame oil
$1/4$ cup raw tahini
1 tablespoon lime juice
2 tablespoons chopped fresh ginger

SAUCE
$1/2$ cup nama shoyu
2 tablespoons raw agave
2 tablespoons fresh lime juice
1 tablespoon sesame oil
Pinch dried chile flakes

ASSEMBLY
3 cups torn spinach
$1 1/2$ teaspoons sesame oil
$3/4$ teaspoon finely diced fresh ginger
Pinch sea salt
$1/4$ teaspoon chili powder
$1/2$ teaspoon sesame seeds
2 cups Sesame-Cashew Filling (see left)
1 cup finely diced carrot
$1/2$ cup finely diced scallions
1 cup finely diced celery
Chives

WRAPPERS Blend 1 cup coconut meat, a pinch salt, and beet juice in a Vita-Mix until very smooth. Spread mixture in a thin even layer over a Teflex sheet and dehydrate 3 hours. Repeat process separately with carrot and spinach juices. Trim edges and cut into 9 squares. Store in plastic wrap in the refrigerator until ready to use. Remove wrappers from refrigerator and allow them to come to room temperature prior to use.

FILLING Process all ingredients in a food processor to a chunky consistency.

SAUCE Combine all ingredients in a medium-size bowl and whisk until well combined.

ASSEMBLY Toss the spinach with the sesame oil, ginger, salt, chili powder, and sesame seeds. Allow to marinate 1 hour; or spread on Teflex sheet, cover with plastic wrap, and place in a dehydrator at 118 degrees F for 10–15 minutes. In a bowl, mix filling, carrot, scallions, and celery. Lay out dumpling wrappers on a workspace and place a small amount of spinach on each. Top with 1 tablespoon filling mixture. Pull up edges around filling to form a beggar's purse and tie with a half chive. Serve with sauce. YIELDS 24

empadinhas de queijo: "cheese" empanadas

These are addictively tasty and surprisingly cheeselike. Although these are more like tartlets, their character is derived from empanadas. Try eating only one—and good luck with that!

SHELLS

2 cups pine nuts, soaked 1–2 hours
2 tablespoons nutritional yeast
1/2 teaspoon salt
1/2 cup water

FILLING

1/2 cup coconut meat
2/3 cup cashews, soaked 1–2 hours

1/3 cup Irish moss
1/4 cup water
1 teaspoon sea salt
1 teaspoon nutritional yeast
1 tablespoon fresh lemon juice
1 tablespoon yellow pepper powder, optional
1/2 teaspoon dried oregano

SHELLS Pulse nuts in a food processor to break up. Add yeast, salt, and water; blend until smooth. Spread in small plastic-lined tart shells; dehydrate 24 hours.

FILLING Blend all ingredients except dried oregano in a Vita-Mix until completely smooth. Pulse in dried oregano. Pour into tart crusts. SERVES 4–6

meaning and reality were
not hidden somewhere
behind things, they were in them, in all of them.

—Hermann Hesse

meaningful

It was well into my raw food journey that I realized my personal preferences were mostly aligned with the Sattvic Diet, which is traditionally defined as pure, clean, and wholesome. Individuals have their own needs and tastes, and I understand that my approach may not be best for everyone; but when I learned the history behind it, food as a whole began to make more sense to me. Understanding our relationship with food is a lifelong pursuit, and being a chef can complicate that learning process even more. In addition to our own choices, we are faced with countless historic, family, and social traditions, as well as others that we pick up along the way in our own lives.

While raw food as a whole does not have many long-standing traditions, its influence is firmly connected to many foods of years past, both vegetarian and otherwise. Many people are aware of a connection between spirituality and vegetarianism but are not always aware of the reason for that. Over time, my style of raw food has become influenced by three factors: seasonal ingredients, various forms of art, and history. Food has meaning to everyone throughout the world, and in order for it to be significant, it should share one of the many connections we form in our lives. Because of this, I like to remain focused on the influences behind food and what it means to those who enjoy it, in terms of both their experience and, ultimately, their memory.

A meal can serve as a reminder of nearly anything in life—good fortune, a New Year's celebration, breaking a fast, long life, love, and much more. While I take liberty with how to actually prepare the recipes, they are quite often grounded by their connection to these meanings.

Many of the recipes in this chapter are based on very classic recipes while others are loose interpretations, but all share the same value of respect for tradition and meaning when sharing a meal.

zaru somen and sweet dashi sake broth

Zaru noodles are named for the slatted box they are traditionally served in and are a Japanese New Year's favorite, symbolic of long life. The coconut "noodles" in this recipe are so durable that they are able to carry the intense but light flavors of the broth. The night this was on a menu I prepared, I had three bowls and was full for the night.

BROTH
1 cup water
1 cup nama shoyu
2 tablespoons dried dulse
1 tablespoon dried wakame
$1/4$ cup brown rice vinegar
2 tablespoons raw agave
1 tablespoon fresh lime juice

SOMEN
2 cups young Thai coconut meat
2 tablespoons black sesame seeds
$1^1/2$ teaspoons shichimi spice
2 tablespoons finely sliced scallion

BROTH Blend water, nama shoyu, dulse, and wakame in a blender until smooth. Strain through a fine sieve into a medium-size bowl. Whisk in remaining ingredients. Store in refrigerator until ready to serve. When ready to serve, pour $1/4$ cup broth in the bottom of two small serving bowls.

SOMEN Slice coconut meat into very thin, uniform noodles. Place equal amounts of coconut noodles in each serving bowl with broth. Top each with a sprinkle of black sesame seeds, shichimi, and scallion. Serve immediately. SERVES 4

ba bao fan blessing eight-treasure "rice": candied fruits with "longan" syrup

Eight treasure rice is a Chinese New Year's favorite, prepared to bring in good spirits and fortune. It is a pudding-like dessert typically made with eight types of freshly dried fruits and sometimes lotus seeds. I loved the festive look of this dish, not to mention the great flavor.

SWEET "RICE"
2 cups jicama, chopped
1 cup pine nuts, soaked for one hour
$1/2$ cup agave nectar
1 tablespoon vanilla
2 tablespoons coconut oil

FRUITS AND NUTS
$1/2$ cup dried cherries, rehydrated
$1/2$ cup golden raisins
$1/2$ cup diced lychee or mango
$1/2$ cup chopped almonds
$1/2$ cup chopped pistachios

$1/2$ cup thinly sliced dried apricots
1 cup agave

"LONGAN" SYRUP
1 cup agave
1 teaspoon minced ginger
$1/2$ cup diced lychee or mango

ASSEMBLY
$1/4$ cup coconut oil
$1/4$ cup very fine julienne of orange zest
$1/2$ cup dried coconut flakes

SWEET "RICE" Pulse jicama and pine nuts in food processor until they have a ricelike consistency. Squeeze out excess water and dehydrate on Teflex sheets for $1\frac{1}{2}$ hours. Add remaining ingredients.

FRUITS AND NUTS Combine all ingredients.

SYRUP Blend ingredients well in a Vita-Mix.

ASSEMBLY Line small bowl with plastic wrap—lightly oil the wrap with coconut oil. Press fruits and nuts all over the wrap and then "rice" firmly on top. Allow to rest for 10 minutes, invert, and remove plastic wrap. Top with orange zest and coconut flakes. Serve with syrup. SERVES 4–6

mochi "ice cream": goji berry, vanilla lemongrass, green tea

Mochi means "rice cake," and they are another traditional New Year's food, due to their resemblance of the mirror decorating the Shinto Shrine. They are a traditional Japanese food at holidays and festivals, including January 11, which is called "Mirror Opening Day." The origin of the name has three translated meanings, including "full moon," "from God," and "stickiness."

MOCHI
1 cup cashews, soaked 1–2 hours
$3/4$ cup young Thai coconut meat
$1/4$ cup raw agave
$1/4$ cup raw coconut oil
Pinch sea salt
$1/4$ teaspoon nonalcohol vanilla extract
Few drops nonalcohol almond extract
$1/2$ cup oat flour*
$3/4$ cup coconut flour**

GOJI BERRY "ICE CREAM"
$1/2$ cup cashews, soaked 1–2 hours
$1/2$ cup macadamia nuts, soaked 1–2 hours
$1/2$ cup young Thai coconut meat
$3/4$ cup raw agave nectar
$1^1/2$ cups water
2 teaspoons nonalcohol vanilla extract
1 teaspoon fresh lemon juice
Pinch sea salt
$1/2$ cup coconut oil
1 cup soaked goji berries, blended and strained
   through a fine sieve

VANILLA LEMONGRASS "ICE CREAM"
$1/2$ cup cashews, soaked 1–2 hours
$1/2$ cup macadamia nuts, soaked 1–2 hours
$1/2$ cup young Thai coconut meat
$3/4$ cup raw agave nectar
$1^1/2$ cups water
2 teaspoons nonalcohol vanilla extract
$1/4$ vanilla bean, scraped
$1/4$ cup lemongrass juice
Pinch sea salt
$1/2$ cup coconut oil

MOCHI Blend first 7 ingredients in a Vita-Mix until very smooth and creamy. Transfer mixture to a medium-size bowl and stir in flours until it is very well combined and lumps are smoothed out. Line a 9 x 13-inch pan with plastic wrap on bottom and sides. Pour dough into prepared pan and spread very thin, approximately $1/2$ inch thick. Place in freezer until firm.

*NOTE: Oat flour is made by grinding whole raw oat groats in a high-speed blender or a coffee or spice grinder, until a very fine flour is achieved.

**NOTE: Coconut flour is made by grinding dried coconut flakes in a high-speed blender or a coffee or spice grinder, until a fine flour is achieved. Do not overprocess or the oils in the coconut will cause the coconut to cake.

GOJI BERRY "ICE CREAM" Blend all ingredients in Vita-Mix until very smooth. Pour into an ice cream maker and follow manufacturer's instructions; or freeze base in a square pan, cut, and run through a masticating juicer (such as the Champion or Greenstar). Freeze overnight. Scoop 2 large rounded scoops of "ice cream" into a pan or plate; freeze until very firm.

VANILLA LEMONGRASS "ICE CREAM" Blend all ingredients in Vita-Mix until very smooth. Pour into ice cream maker and follow manufacturer's instructions; or freeze base in square pan, cut, and run through masticating juicer (such as the Champion or Greenstar). Freeze overnight. Scoop 2 large rounded scoops of "ice cream" into pan or plate; freeze until very firm.

GREEN TEA "ICE CREAM"

$1/2$ cup cashews, soaked 1–2 hours
$1/2$ cup macadamia nuts, soaked 1–2 hours
$1/2$ cup young Thai coconut meat
$1/2$ cup raw agave
$1^1/2$ cups water
2 teaspoons nonalcohol vanilla extract
$2^1/2$ tablespoons green tea powder
Pinch sea salt
$1/2$ cup coconut oil

BLACK CACAO SYRUP

$1^1/2$ cups raw agave
$1/2$ cup raw cacao powder
2 tablespoons raw carob powder
$1/4$ teaspoon nonalcohol vanilla extract
Pinch sea salt
$1/2$ cup coconut oil

ASSEMBLY

Oat flour
Mint or basil sprigs

GREEN TEA "ICE CREAM" Blend all ingredients in Vita-Mix until very smooth. Pour into ice cream maker and follow manufacturer's instructions; or freeze base in square pan, cut, and run through masticating juicer (such as the Champion or Greenstar). Freeze overnight. Scoop 2 large rounded scoops of ice cream into pan or plate; freeze until very firm.

BLACK CACAO SYRUP Blend all ingredients in a blender until smooth. Keep in a warm area until ready to serve.

ASSEMBLY Dust a dry cutting board with oat flour. Turn out frozen mochi onto cutting board and peel off plastic. Cut six 4 x 4-inch pieces. With floured hands, flatten each piece until very thin. Place 1 scoop of ice cream in the center of each mochi sheet and mold mochi around ice cream until ice cream is completely covered; smooth ridges with fingers.

Place mochi-covered ice cream in freezer immediately and freeze 8–10 hours until completely frozen. To serve, slice ends off each mochi ice cream ball and cut into 2 uniform pieces. Place a slice of each flavor on serving plates and garnish with mint or basil sprigs and cacao syrup. SERVES 4

cold spicy long-life noodles with ginger sauce

Chinese noodles symbolize a long life and good health, and therefore should be served very long. Peanuts are actually very rarely available raw, but we were able to find raw peanuts from our friends at rawfood.com that are now available and are excellent in dishes requiring an interesting textural note.

NOODLES
2 large jicama, cut into long noodles with a spiralizer
$1/2$ cup roughly chopped wild raw peanuts
$1/4$ cup sliced scallions (cut into thin 1-inch slices)
$1/2$ cup mung bean sprouts
1 cup roughly chopped bok choy

SAUCE
$1/4$ cup sesame oil
$1/4$ cup soy sauce
$1/4$ cup fresh lemon juice
$1/4$ cup tahini
2 tablespoons raw agave
2 tablespoons minced ginger

NOODLES Mix all ingredients by hand.

SAUCE Blend all ingredients well in a Vita-Mix.

ASSEMBLY Toss the noodles with the sauce several times until well coated and serve. SERVES 4

vietnamese pho broth with tofu

Pho is the national soup of Vietnam, where it is universally loved. It is also very popular in the United States. There are many theories about its creation—it was invented in the early part of the twentieth century and was influenced by both French and Chinese traditions. Some even claim that its name came from *feu,* derived from the French word for fire, as in *pot-au-feu,* which the French colonialists introduced in Vietnam.

BROTH

$1/2$ cup nama shoyu
2 tablespoons lemongrass juice
$1/4$ cup fresh lime juice
$1/2$ cup olive oil
2 cups celery juice
$1/2$ cup carrot juice
$1/2$ cup apple juice
Black pepper
1 teaspoon red pepper flakes
$1/2$ cup raw agave
1 tablespoon diced red onion
$1/2$ teaspoon star anise
1 chipotle chile, soaked
1 tablespoon miso
2 tablespoons chopped dulse

TOFU

1 cup cashews, soaked 1–2 hours
$1/2$ cup fresh young Thai coconut meat
$1/2$ cup raw carrageenan*
$1/4$ cup water
$1/4$ teaspoon sea salt

ASSEMBLY

$1/2$ cup very fine, long zucchini noodles
$1/2$ cup very thin coconut noodles
$1/4$ cup mung bean sprouts
2 tablespoons thinly sliced scallions (sliced on a diagonal)
$1/4$ cup very thinly sliced red bell pepper
$1/4$ cup chopped cashews
1 tablespoon black sesame seeds
$1/4$ cup cilantro leaves

BROTH Blend all ingredients except dulse in a Vita-Mix, then place in a large container. Add dulse and dehydrate 6–8 hours; strain.

TOFU Line the bottom and sides of a small pan or square container with plastic wrap. Drain cashews. Blend all ingredients in a Vita-Mix until completely smooth. Pour into a lined pan (tofu should be about 1 $1/2$ inches thick) and cover with plastic wrap. Refrigerate about 2 hours until firm. When ready to serve, remove tofu from container by lifting plastic wrap out of pan and gently transferring tofu to a cutting board. Cut into $1/2$-inch squares with a butter knife.

*NOTE: Raw carrageenan is prepared by soaking salt-packed Irish moss until all salt is removed. Soak Irish moss overnight, then blend with an equal amount of water until smooth. Store in refrigerator for up to 1 week.

ASSEMBLY Warm pho broth in a dehydrator for 30 minutes. Place half the vegetables in the bottom of soup bowls and top with broth. Pour broth into soup bowls and top with tofu, remaining vegetables, black sesame seeds, and cilantro leaves. SERVES 4

fortune cookies

I added fortune cookies to our Chinese-inspired menu, not fully expecting that my sous chefs Kristen and Anna would be able to actually find a way to make them. Lo and behold, they were perfectly executed. Interestingly, fortune cookies are a California—not a Chinese—invention. They remain a lighthearted and fun way to end the meal, hopefully with a welcoming prophecy.

1 1/4 cups flax meal
3/4 cup chopped pear
1/2 cup young coconut meat
2 teaspoons lemon juice

1/3 cup maple syrup
1/2 teaspoon salt
1 teaspoon vanilla
1 cup water

Blend all ingredients in a Vita-mix except water until smooth. Add water until batter is pasty but still thick. Spread into 3-inch circles on Teflex sheets and dehydrate 6–8 hours until firm but still pliable. Place a fortune note on top of each cookie with the end of note barely hanging over the edge. Carefully transfer to dehydrator trays and form into fortune cookie shapes, by folding in half, and then folding again to pull down pointed edges. Use paper clips to secure edges if needed. Dehydrate another 18–24 hours until crisp. YIELDS 2 DOZEN

spicy "fried" spring rolls with sweet tamarind fondue

Spring rolls, so named because they are typically eaten during Chinese festivals in the spring, are normally filled with crispy vegetables and sometimes cabbage or mushrooms. They are not always vegetarian, but quite often are. The wrapper in this recipe makes use of one of my favorite techniques and embraces, rather than overpowers, the filling.

WRAPPERS
2 cups flax meal
2 cups chopped yellow squash
1 cup chopped coconut meat
2 tablespoons fresh lemon juice
4 cups water
1/4 cup raw agave nectar
1 teaspoon sea salt
1 teaspoon ground coriander
1 teaspoon ground cumin
2 scallions, thinly sliced on a diagonal

FILLING
1 cup julienned carrots
1/4 cup sliced scallions
1 cup shredded Napa cabbage
1 1/2 cups dried shiitake mushrooms,
    soaked 1 hour and dehydrated 2 hours
1/2 teaspoon salt
Black pepper
1/4 cup olive oil

TOFU
1 cup cashews, soaked 1–2 hours
1/2 cup fresh young Thai coconut meat

1/2 cup raw carrageenan (see page 132)
1/4 cup water
1/4 teaspoon sea salt
1 1/2 teaspoons ancho chile powder
1/4 teaspoon cayenne
1/4 cup cilantro

CHILE SAUCE
3/4 teaspoon chipotle chile powder
2 cups cashews, soaked 1–2 hours
1/4 teaspoon salt
1/4 cup nama shoyu
1/4 cup plus 1 tablespoon water

SWEET TAMARIND FONDUE
1 cup dried tamarind paste
1/2 cup raw agave
3 tablespoons lime juice
1/4 cup coconut water
2 tablespoons water
1/2 teaspoon salt

GARNISH
Cilantro leaves

WRAPPERS Blend all ingredients except scallions in a Vita-Mix until smooth; stir in scallions. Spread thinly into 6- to 7-inch rounds on dehydrator Teflex sheets. Dehydrate 5–6 hours until dry but very pliable.

FILLING Fold all ingredients together.

TOFU Line the bottom and sides of a small pan or square container with plastic wrap. Blend all ingredients except cilantro in Vita-Mix until completely smooth; stir in cilantro. Pour into lined pan (tofu should be about 1 1/2 inches thick); cover with plastic wrap. Refrigerate about 2 hours until firm. Remove tofu from container by lifting plastic wrap out of pan and gently transferring to a cutting board. Cut tofu into 2-inch squares with a butter knife.

CHILE SAUCE Blend all ingredients in Vita-Mix until smooth.

SWEET TAMARIND FONDUE Blend all ingredients well in Vita-Mix. Strain through a chinois.

ASSEMBLY Fold the chile sauce into spring roll filling, add tofu, and adjust seasoning. Place a large tablespoon of filling on each spring roll wrapper and spread it out in a row. Fold wrappers tightly. To serve, cut each wrapper on a bias lengthwise, lean one against the other, and garnish with Sweet Tamarind Fondue and cilantro leaves. SERVES 4

thai cucumber salad

One of my first experiences with Thai cuisine was during an early chef position I held at a Brazilian restaurant. One evening, I wasn't feeling well and one of the talented cooks, Laisoon Saetio, made a spicy Thai soup with rice. On other occasions, he would prepare cucumber salads with lots of mint and toasted peanuts to go with heartier dishes. In time, the entire kitchen staff would line up for his delicious meals—he and I went on to work together for many years, and this dish is a reminder of his great talent and warm, gentle personality.

SALAD
1/4 cup roughly chopped basil
2 medium cucumbers, quartered lengthwise and thinly
   sliced
1 head butter or Bibb lettuce, torn into small pieces
1 yellow bell pepper, julienned
1 teaspoon salt
1/4 cup mint leaves

DRESSING
3/4 cup sesame oil
1/2 cup nama shoyu

1/4 cup olive oil
1/4 cup lime juice
1 tablespoon maple syrup
3 Thai chiles or 3 teaspoons red chile flakes
1/4 cup cashew butter
Water as needed to thin

GARNISH
1/3 cup chopped cashews
2 tablespoons sesame oil
1/4 cup diced red pepper

SALAD Combine all salad ingredients in a bowl.

DRESSING Blend all ingredients until smooth in a Vita-Mix.

ASSEMBLY Dress salad generously with dressing and top with cashews, oil, and red pepper. SERVES 4

index

Metric Conversion Chart

Volume Measurements		Weight Measurements		Temperature Conversion	
U.S.	Metric	U.S.	Metric	Fahrenheit	Celsius
1 teaspoon	5 ml	1/2 ounce	15 g	250	120
1 tablespoon	15 ml	1 ounce	30 g	300	150
1/4 cup	60 ml	3 ounces	90 g	325	160
1/3 cup	75 ml	4 ounces	115 g	350	180
1/2 cup	125 ml	8 ounces	225 g	375	190
2/3 cup	150 ml	12 ounces	350 g	400	200
3/4 cup	175 ml	1 pound	450 g	425	220
1 cup	250 ml	2 1/4 pounds	1 kg	450	230